Coventry Market

In A Round About Way

Pete Chambers

This book is dedicated to all the 'nice' people who ever worked or shopped in Coventry Market, you know who you are.

Why a book?

I joined Coventry Market in the summer of 1995 and I have looked forward to coming in to work everyday since, there is a buzz about Coventry Market unpredictability, a vibrant atmosphere and excitement, not knowing who you will meet or what you will find to buy. It's where friends meet or where you can just come for a chat and be part of a big family. The Market has weathered well over the years and has adapted and met the challenges that the city has faced, from the boom town of the manufacturing 60s and 70s to periods of economic troubles with a declining car industry and now the growth of an interest in local fresh produce the Market continues to meet them all. There is no other building within the city that has so many stories to tell and reflects the history of the community of Coventry so completely.

This book hopefully documents the stories and the characters that are the life of Coventry Market from that day in 1958 when a unique circular building was given to the people of Coventry.

To me, my first memories of the Market are being 7 years old and Aunty Betty dragging me and my sister through crowded isles to get to the toy stall, the Market being so busy with rushing streams of people on a Saturday you were lucky not to get swept away. As a child you had never seen so many people in one place, sights, smells and colours that were exciting and alien. I would always have to borrow extra pocket money from Aunty Betty to buy those toys and to this day I have never paid her back. Later on it was the straight-legged rockabilly jeans from Deakin's and biker jackets from Howard Sweet's leather stalls. And of course everyone in the world seems to have a memory of riding the roundabout scrambling to get on at the front of the ship with the bell or the top of the cowboy wagon it was the perfect place to come shopping.

So, why a book? I know Pete has a love for Coventry and a love for Coventry Market and I think its important that we try to document at least the spirit of what Coventry Market was like in the funny round building that you always got lost in.

I asked him to pull all the stories together and collect the memories whilst we can still remember them and whilst many of the characters are still about. It's a great opportunity to celebrate the Market and the people who continue to make it a very special place to be.

Brian Sexton, Market Manager

Above, the author Pete Chambers, collecting information in the 1958 style Market Parlour. Below, Market Manager Brian Sexton and Hazel O'Connor.

Market Research

The phrase ' A unique shopping experience' is becoming increasingly applied to a plethora of bog standard and to be honest, mostly forgettable shopping centres (or shopping malls as we are increasingly calling them for some inexplicable reason). Let's face it, take any high street anywhere in the British Isles, and the names you will see will pretty much all be the same (well the ones still surviving the dreaded credit crunch that is). Unique it aint, an experience, well possibly, not *necessarily* a good one though. Now, I'm not here to have a dig at our shops and chain stores, but their slave to conformity and big business is becoming a trifle obvious and lacking vision or originality.

So about now, you would expect me to begin an sycophantic diatribe, extolling the virtues of Coventry Market, and cracking on about what a unique experience shopping there can be. Well, there is some truth in that, there again we are talking about a product of the 1950's here. Despite it's charms, this concrete doughnut of a market has become tired and has resigned itself that pretty soon, it will be residing in retail heaven right next to Owen Owen and Woolworth's (not if the Grade II Listing stays it won't). When that happens, and a brand new market will be built hopefully and we will see that in reality it's the people who shop and work in the market, rather than the building that gives the 'character' to the place. I spend a lot of time in the market (it's now becoming slightly unhealthy, but I'm having counselling for it though). The point is, there are some great human beings in this place, genuine, salt of the earth good people. Every time I go in it's an education, you always learn something new. Not all of it instantly useful I must confess, but at it's least interesting and at its best, fascinating. Let's be honest, you don't get a shopping experience like this anywhere else in Coventry. That's why you seldom hear a bad word about the place. It's not perfect of course, but it is ours and we all feel that it's a little glimpse of a Coventry of the past. Where people mattered, and interaction with the customer was an act of everyday social intercourse, not some scheme to make more money.

This book is not trying to be some in-depth history of Coventry Market, it's more about me finding out about the place, and happily passing that information on. It's about a moment in time, a snapshot of something about to disappear for good and now is the best time to take a closer look. A huge pat on the back to Market Manager Brian "are you still here" Sexton, who commissioned me to write this book and who had the vision to get the urban everyday history of the place documented at this moment in time.

So it's on with the show.

Pete Chambers

Coventry Market-All kinds of everything.

HISTORY

Before it was a round

This book is a look at the present Coventry Market or 'the round one'. We can't however approach the subject of Coventry markets without mentioning the places of market retail that came before it.

So lets get all historic for a while. The market is the oldest undertaking possessed by Coventry City Council, dating back to the Charter of Edward III on 11th April 1346. Although records show that markets were held in the 12th century, divided into the Prior's Half and the Earl's Half, the two sections were divided by Priory Row.

Originally the market was held at "Cross Cheaping", the word "cheaping" actually signifying "market". It began as a number of street side benches where traders sold their wares. As it grew so did the problem of congestion and overcrowding. In 1719 a new Market house was erected, where 15 stalls were let to 13 tenants for a rent of £2 per year. This was in use until 1867.

In the early 19th century Friday remained the chief market day, although there were also markets on Wednesdays and Saturdays. Markets for various commodities were held in different parts of the town.

The old market hall demolished in 1867
Photo courtesy of Coventry City Libraries

In 1822 the market for cattle, sheep and pigs that had previously been held in the open at Gosford Street, was replaced by a cattle market at the top of Bishop Street. Whilst a 'beast' market for sheep and pigs took place in Cook Street.

In 1922 the Corporation acquired the old barracks site, and an open-air retail and wholesale market was established there. Come 1936 The Barracks Market (known locally as China-Town) became a covered affair. Meanwhile, the Smithfield Market, originally a cattle market, gave way to meat in 1919 to become a general market. Between 1919 and 1921 it was utilized for the sale of crocks at the annual Great Fair. It closed in 1933. The Second World War saw Coventry down but never out, and the heart-breaking destruction of Godiva's fair city inevitably extended to it's markets. The Barracks Market was severely damaged in the onslaught and this saw the West Orchard Market established to ease the problem. That was replaced in 1953 by the Rex Market in Corporation Street and two years later, the Barras Heath Wholesale Market was opened in the Stoke Heath area of the city.

So, with the reconstruction of the city following the Second World War, a new market was commissioned, something that was radical and new. The new market would be circular and incorporate a roof car park. Every possible effort was made to make the market as convenient as possible to both traders and shoppers. The plans were thoroughly discussed and agreed with the stall holders' Committee. The circular shape was to ensure as far as possible equal trading facilities on all parts of the market as well as giving it a distinctive character in contrast with surrounding buildings. The project cost £385,000 and when it opened on 4th November 1958, most gave it the thumbs up. "It's fine, the best we have ever been in" declared fruit stall holder Mrs E Wallace. "A grand place, more like an exhibition than anything else, I like it very much" said Mr William Parkinson who had a stall selling arts and craft goods on it!

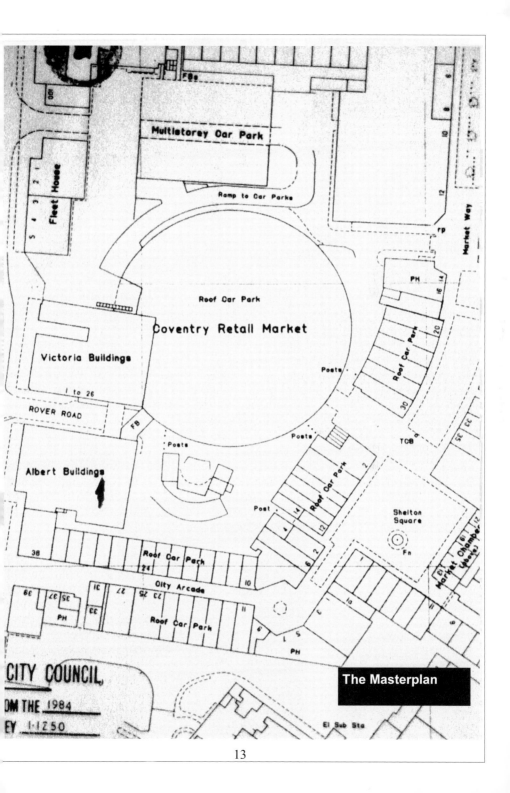

The Masterplan

13

Round round get around I get around.

So it came to pass that the people of Coventry woke on the morning of November 4th 1958 and there it was, a vision of roundness, standing all majestic in it's concrete loveliness, behold Coventry's newest icon, all hail Coventry Market.

The new market was opened by her Royal Highness Princess Alexandra of Kent. After a slight delay (the Prin-

Under construction

cess' train was eight minutes late) she eventually made her way to the market. Speaking from a make-shift stage in the centre of the building, along side the Lord Mayor Alderman H.H.K.Winslow J.P., she paid tribute to the city. Saying, "This great city which is famous throughout the world for it's heroic spirit in the darkest years of the war". The 21 year-old Princess said "she was glad to have some small part in the realisation of this great new venture".

While Councillor E. M. Rogers, Chairman of The Market and Baths Committee, added, "In olden days the market was an important focal centre for the community. We hope that in this new market, with its teabars, its children's roundabout,

COVENTRY MARKET

      ❋ ❋ ❋

Officially Opened

by

Her Royal Highness

PRINCESS ALEXANDRA

OF KENT

❋ ❋ ❋

Tuesday, 4th November, 1958

and in this central concourse where we are gathered, Coventry Citizens will again find something of the traditional market atmosphere which has been part of our way of life for so many centuries".

The new market incorporated 160 island stalls, 40 shop stalls, pitching stalls on the perimeter and two meat shops within the market. There were two internal tea bars and another outside. The fish market comprised of 14 fish stalls, with ancillary storage accommodation. The storage basement comprised of 78 storage compartments.

The Princess and Councillor F.M Rogers

The roof car park was a big talking point at the time. It had room for 200 cars and wait for this one boys and girls, an electrically heated ramp to avoid any difficulties with snow or ice! No wonder they hyped up the car park, this was state of the art in 1958, actually it would be state of the art in 2009 come to think of it. Indeed both the heated ramp and the roof car park were unique innovations at the time.

The circular design was unique and a stroke of genius. With its seven entrances around the building, it gave all stall holders an equal crack at the retail whip.

Photo courtesy of the Coventry Telegraph

Its circular design also ensured that once inside the building, shoppers were encouraged to circulate (literally), rather than just heading straight to their objective. This works on a grander scale too. It's surprising that even with this 'all in one' out of town supermarket shopping mentality, I hear of so many people who still come to the market to buy their fruit and vegetables and a host of many other products. This has to have a knock-on effect with the city's commerce as a whole, drawing in those market shoppers and exiting them at several points, thus benefiting many other shops in the city centre. If you think of it, a round market makes sense in every way, yet it would seem that Coventry's Retail Market is the only one of that type certainly in Europe, if not the world (stand by for the letters to come in on this one).

Right in the centre of the building covering the 37 foot (11.277 6 meters) roof diameter is the domed canopy, or the 'eye' of the market. It was designed (along with the peripheral windows) to give natural light. Beneath this centre piece there stands a mosaic, provided by members of the Association of Building Technicians, a series of bench seats were installed here for the customers use.

Then there was the fish market, people get very animated over the fish market. Is it because it's the last bastion of a more genteel way of life, when long before the days of Cap'in Birdy and his frozen crumb, there was wet fish? I personally think it went down-hill when they removed 'out-doors' from public houses, at least wet fish has not gone the same way and disappeared altogether. Anyway back to 1958, and the fish market was a sight to behold. The seven pillars in the market were surrounded at it's upper most section by four ornate figures. They were King Neptune, a sailor dancing the hornpipe and two mermaids to presumably keep them company. A Mr James Brown of the City Architects department was responsible for the design.

This was the first market to be built in Britain since the war and the initial feedback looked good, but once the novelty of a circular market had worn off, trade began to slow right down, and surprisingly that first 12 months became a struggle. This was due in part to the construction work taking place all around the site, with many potential shoppers finding it hard to access the market or amazingly, not being able to find it at all!

A newspaper report quoted Former Chairman of the Market Traders Federation Ken Littlewood on that first year. "The first twelve months were dicey" he said, "but there wasn't another market like it in the country at the time, and in my view there still isn't". Toy stall holder Madeline Walker was just eleven when the market opened and remembers getting a day off school "My Uncle Ted had a high class fruit stall and I helped him move in" she says. "He had a fistful of brand new pennies that he threw to the children after the opening ceremony. It was tough for a while", Madeline recalled. She reckons it was only the hula-hoop craze of the following summer that saved her parents toy stall from closure.

The project takes shape

The market as you would never see it again. All ready for stock.

Above-The mosaic in construction, and below, finished in place in the market .

Save Our Market, that was then, but this is now

We tend to take things a lot for granted when all is well and even something as iconic as the market, is often used and thought little of, until the next shopping trip. That's until a threat looms that promises to change the very structure of our lives, or much less dramatically to our beloved market.

A proposal was drawn up by the City Council in 1998, that saw the scrapping of the round market, and seeing the stalls move to the Lower Precinct. The Council misjudged the mood of the market shoppers and traders, and they soon became the less-than-happy owners of a 25,000 signature petition. The people had spoken, and proved without doubt, that the market was that important to the people of Coventry.

The Coventry Telegraph letter's page was virtually given over to the debate, with angry readers putting pen to paper. "Please leave our market alone. We don't want it moved or altered. We love it and the market traders are wonderful people", said D Shone from Allesley. Whilst S Dunk had this to say, "Leave Coventry Market where it is. We don't need more shops, but we do need variety". One rather good letter by Michael Smith begged the question, "I am fascinated to know how 223 stalls are supposed to fit in the space available. Even one of the city's finest journalists, Chris Arnot had much to say in the Telegraph, ending an extremely well reasoned article with, "Councillors would do well not to underestimate the love Coventry people nurture for their market-in-the round". He was of course right and a rethink was hastily thrown on the table, finally dropping the demolition idea altogether. The people and Coventry Market, not to mention common sense, had won.

The Market, worth saving?

It does make me think though, that if such a campaign would be so strongly supported nowadays? Although it has to be said that of late, I think many of the traders would be more than happy to move to a new modern purpose built site as part of the Council's multi-Billion Pound regeneration scheme.

Well, it was around the time I wrote the above, that the English Heritage Grade II Listing was placed on the market, this time there was support alright, but the majority were in favour of not saving the market, so it turned out to be very prophetic words really.

Mural-The writing was on the wall.

The Market mural has for many years been mainly ignored by most, that was until it became the core catalyst for the preservation of Coventry Market and the subsequent Grade II Listing that followed. It was unveiled in June 1961 by the then Lord Mayor Alderman W Callow and formally handed over by Herr Heinz Kursitza a Dresden City Council worker and Director of the workers and peasants faculty at the city's University. He said he bought greetings from the Lord Mayor of Dresden and all the citizens and said it would emphasise the links between our two cities (Coventry was twinned with Dresden in 1959). Councillor W Spencer, Chairman of the Markets and Baths Committee, said that no incoming Chairman had ever had such a historic opening to his year of office.

Originally the mural was 100 feet long and five feet high and designed by East German Herr Jurgens Seidel who was a teacher at a technical college in Dresden. The design was one of five submitted by German artists in a Dresden competition for a prize winning design for Coventry Market. The mural were painted by Herr Seidel in Dresden on plywood panel. Each of the ten panels depicting various industries and crafts.

The mural was removed in July 1998 as part of the £1.2 million revamp and it got its second unveiling in November 1998. Word has it that some of the art-work was missing on its return. Of course this was pre-listing, so it was of little significance then, just try doing it now however and you would probably be publicly hanged.

Part of the famous mural that now presides around the market office area.

Leslie Walker– a man who turned it a-round

In May 1969 Leslie Walker retired as General Manager of Markets for Coventry Corporation after 25 years. He was a legendary Manager. When he took the job the city centre was in ruins and the Barracks Market had lost its roof and shops in the old City Arcade had windows boarded up and 'peep-hole' displays in them. He did the best he could and patched things up, eventually opening a temporary market at West Orchards on the Market Hall site (until The Hotel Leofric claimed the site). He was responsible for the Barras Wholesale Market in Stoke Heath, that opened on 4th July 1955, though many market traders protested at being sent into the 'wilderness' to collect their fruit and veg.

It was Leslie Walker who pressed for a market in-the-round, and saw his dream come alive in 1958. He wanted to move away from the square market format, where traders on end stalls and outside stalls had the best of the trade and rents being charged in relation to this. In a circular market, nobody can claim the best pitch, indeed pitches were chosen by the then Lord Mayor picking out traders names at random and the National President picking the random stall number.

On his retirement Leslie said, "It's been an exciting job, with never a dull moment". Before becoming Market manager Mr Walker had played at half-back for Derby County for a few seasons, alongside Harry Storer, who became a manager of Coventry City of course. He was also National President of the Institute of Market Officers in 1965 and completed an amazing 40 years in market administration. On top of that he was also a lay preacher for 40 years.

On his retirement he was replaced by new Market Manager Mr. Harry Phipps. Leslie was a hard act to follow and Coventry will probably never see his like again. Having said that, present Market Managers Brian Sexton and Michael Finnegan are doing a pretty good job between them.

The legendary Leslie Walker
Courtesy of the Coventry Telegraph

Some original market traders, but how many are still trading?

Harry Aber Ltd-*Drapery, Hoisery, Fancy Goods and Underwear*
S.H Abington Ltd-*Outfitters*
M Alouf-Household Linens and Hoisery
A.B.C-*Ashers's Bargain Counter*
B.G. Barber-*Fish,Rabbits & Poultry*
Mrs E.Beecham-*Nottingham Laces*
J&M Billies Ltd-*Coats,Costumes,Dresses,etc*
Birch & Sons (Coventry) Ltd-*Books and Antigues*
G.W & A.E. Bott-*General Fruiterer and Greengrocer*
James Cooper & Sons-*Glass and China Dealers*
Louis Crammer-*Jewellery and Fancy Goods*
Donner's-*Grocers,Toilet and Household Goods*
Dunn's Fish Supply-*Fish and Poultry*
A.H.Edwards-*Greengrocer and Fruiterer*
Edwards & Barnett –*Nurserymen*
C.Roy Ellis-*Shoes*
Wm,Hendrige& Sons-*Butchery*
T.C.Hyde-*Butchery*
G.Kilworth Ltd-*Hoisery,Underwear,Knitwear,etc*
Leslie & Son-*Greengrocer and Fruiterer*
Lews-*Fancy Goods and Groceries*
Chas. Mitchell-*Fruiterer*
E.Norton-*Textile,Remnants and Piece Goods*
Old Riley-*Greengrocery*
M.A Pearsons-*Knitting Wools and Accesories*
W..E.Plastow (Retail) Ltd-*Fishmongery*
H.Pindar-*Fish and Poultery*
D.Ram-*Hoisery,Knitwear and Underwear*
Raynors-*Jewellery,Watches & Clocks*
L.Samuels-*Hoisery,Ladies & Gent's Wear*
A.Southall-*Fishmongery and poultry*
Gloria Squires-*Ladies Milliner*
J.Sweet-Costumiers-*Coats & dresses*
The Carpet Stores-*Carpets and Rugs*
G.H.Hayes Co Ltd-*Tripe,Cowheels,Black Pudding and Sundries*
The Ideal Stalls "Jay Ess" Ltd-*Drapers*
The Shoe Kings-*Boots and Shoes*
Percy Wain-*Ladies' and Gent's Footwear*
Wesley's-*Hoisery,Underwear and Outerwear*
Woolf's-*Clothing and Outfitting*

To List or
Not To List

I've Got a Little List

So, I was writing this book about the Market, as you do, all was going as normal then suddenly without as much as an "excuse me", English Heritage decree the place a Grade II Listed building! It's a decision that has well and truly put the cat amongst the pigeons. Most of us had accepted that the place had become tired and was treading water, until the nice man from Jerde came along with a brand new market where all us happy folk could shop and work in. That multimillion pound redevelopment of Coventry City Centre now has to be rewritten and if it does happen, will it mean a brand spanking new development will have an out-dated concrete structure at its heart? As I write plans are unfolding to challenge the listing, It seems that the majority of market traders want to move to a bright new place that has windows, air conditioning in the summer and heating in the winter. I personally feel we should move on, I'm afraid that there are too many grey thinkers in this city, no wonder we get branded a concrete jungle, where's the vision? I'm a Coventry Ambassador and I'm proud of Coventry's history and it should be preserved at all costs, but not when it threatens the total re-fit of this city. A city that quite frankly is tired and is crying out for reinvention and not when many of the elements that give it its Grade II Listing can safely be removed and resited in a new market.

I recently visited Dubai, a City Emirate that is visionary and not frightened to go forward. I stood there one night watching the world's biggest fountains, outside of the world's biggest shopping mall, in front of the world tallest man-made structure. My mind came back to my beloved Coventry, oh to have just a tiny piece of that wow-factor in my own city I thought, but even if we had the money would we do it? Or would the grey thinkers tell us that this is Coventry and we don't do things like that here. That's far too tacky, too exciting, too much passion and vision for our liking, what we need is more grey concrete. Maybe when we build the new development and a new market, all the grey thinkers can go and live in the old market, and we can call it Dystopia and watch them standing on the car park roof shouting scorn on our new bright vision.

Coventry Market as Jerde originally saw it, though a new round design is now on the cards, if of course it becomes a reality.

Image Courtesy: The Jerde Partnership

Listed Building Description Coventry Retail Market 18-JUN-09

A market hall built in 1957 to designs by Douglas Beaton, Ralph Iredale and Ian Crawford of Coventry City Architect's Department.

EXTERIOR: The market consists of a series of concrete arches joined by a ring beam, all left exposed, with brick infilling and a concrete roof, laid out as a car park, with a central circular roof light. It has a circular plan, just over 84m in diameter and 4 ½ m high, is laid out with 160 island stalls, arranged in groups of two or four units in concentric rings, with 40 'shop stalls' set into the perimeter wall, 16 of them facing inwards, and a small circular, glazed attendant's kiosk situated near the main entrance to the south-east side. The basement, under the western half of the building only, is laid out as a delivery and storage area.

INTERIOR: Inside, the circular space is characterised by the tall V-shaped concrete 'columns' that hold the roof. The timber stalls, designed as the traditional 'market table', can be secured after trading by raising the side flaps and by sliding boards into horizontal channels and locking these into position. Some of the original shop and stall signs have survived. Natural light enters via the clerestory windows along the top perimeter of the building and through the clerestory lighting and oculi in the central dome. The space under this dome, designed as an area for shoppers to rest, is lined with seats and has a terrazzo mosaic floor designed by David Embling, with a central sun motif, a gift from the Coventry Branch of the Association of Building Technicians. Two of the adjacent V-shaped roof supports are adorned with a bronze plaque, one commemorating the opening by Princess Alexandra in 1958, and the other listing the names of the members of Coventry's Markets and Baths Committee of 1958-1959. Above the current market office is an impressive painted mural by art students from Dresden commissioned especially for the market in the 1950s in a Socialist Realist manner, depicting farming and industrial scenes. The V-shaped supports near the central dome and the walls near the current fish mongers are decorated with colourful figures of mermaids, sailors and Neptune made by Jim Brown in the late 1950s, and moved here from the former fish market (Victoria Buildings, now demolished).

HISTORY: Coventry's retail market was built in 1957 to designs by Douglas Beaton, Ralph Iredale and Ian Crawford of Coventry City Architect's Department. Tenders were sought in December 1956. In November 1958 it was officially opened by Princess Alexandra (Lady Ogilvy, born 1936). It was claimed to be the first large scale covered market in England erected after the Second World War, that at Wolverhampton, built 1955, being partially open. It was built on the site of Barracks and Rex Markets, which had been partially damaged during the bombing of Coventry in November 1940, to accommodate the former stallholders whilst providing additional facilities.

Jerde's new round Coventry Market design. This looks amazing, do we really want to dismiss this?
Image Courtesy: The Jerde Partnership

27

Various designs were considered, but eventually a circular design was chosen to encourage circulation and to offer a number of entrances. It was given a flat roof in order to create a car park (with a heated ramp to prevent icing, now no longer there), and was to become the central focus for a complex scheme of linked roof car parks in Coventry. A well loved feature of the pre-war market of Coventry had been a children's merry-go-round, designed by David Mason with models of vehicles manufactured in Coventry, which was erected near a café outside the main entrance. This merry-go-round, known as the Coventry Market Roundabout, moved around the site as the market and various adjoining shops opened. It now stands inside the market (it is not fixed and as such is not listed). The market was attached to Victoria Buildings, formerly known as the Ace Works. These engineering works had survived the war and were subsequently converted to a fish market, with its upper floors remaining in use as factories. The cast-iron columns of Victoria Buildings were decorated with the colourful figures by Jim Brown, the City Architect who was responsible for much of Coventry's art work in its new buildings. The fish market was demolished in the late 1990s, and the figures are now situated in Coventry Retail Market.

SOURCES OF ABOVE REPORT

N Pevsner and A Wedgwood, The Buildings of England: Warwickshire, p 272

The Architect and Building News, vol 208, 14 July 1955, pp 38-39.

The Architect and Building News, vol 122, 21 July 1955, p 92.

The Architect and Building News, vol 215, 22 April 1959, pp 508-510.

Architecture and Building, February 1959, pp 62-66.

Official Architecture and Planning, January 1959, pp 28 & 31.

J & C Gould, Coventry Planned - The Architecture of the Plan for Coventry 1940-1978 (unpublished report commissioned by English Heritage, 2009).

Elain Harwood, 'Coventry Retail Market' (unpublished English Heritage report,2008).

So to be fair about all this I thought it would be a good idea to talk to some of the Market people and see how they felt. First up Bill Duffin from Shoekings and The Market Traders Association.

"We were part of the Jerde plan until we found out that English Heritage had Listed our market building, which was a shock to say the least. It's a big round lump of concrete, which is cold in winter and excessively hot in summer, with not a very good disabled access. It's not a very good shopping experience at the moment. It has lasted well 50 years but people expect more nowadays than they did then. We also have no public toilets in here. Unfortunately some of the food stalls do not have proper ventilation and the smell lingers.

This is a building built in the 50's but life has moved on and the public and the traders deserve better. In the new market we could look out on flowing water and green spaces and if it does not happen goodness knows what will. I think it will be listed for another 50 years and we will be here for posterity. It is getting more and more expensive to maintain and are we attracting the amount of people we had 20 or 30 years ago? I just don't know".

Obviously the decision has caused much debate and not all traders welcome a new market. Neil Moran explains why he doesn't want a new market, or indeed English Heritage's involvement.

My point of view in regards to the re-location of the market was and still is, I don't want to move. It's taken thirty years to build up my clientele, who know where I am. They come to me and every week, people will still say "Oh, we got lost" or "Couldn't find you", even though I have been in the same spot for thirty years, so to re-locate me to another building completely, would be for me disaster.

I know the older people, the pensioners, there's no way they would find me again. I know that sounds harsh, but they wouldn't, they struggle to find me now, even though I haven't moved. It's taken a long time to build up that customer base. To be honest, I wouldn't like to move anywhere else in this market and so to a completely new building is a no, no. That's on a personal point of view, however other people who are struggling in here, who don't rely on a regular base, would consider moving to a new building may give us a new foot-fall, which could be doubtful, we don't know.

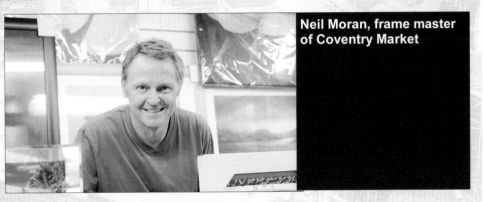

Neil Moran, frame master of Coventry Market

Where as fishmonger Clive Miller sees it like this. "The actual Heritage side to it is not an issue to me, that's just a reason for us not moving, personally If I had the choice I wouldn't have particularly wanted Heritage to get involved with the running of this market. My ideal situation would be tidy this market up, and bring it up this Century and stay as I am.

Personally I think the building should be Grade II listed for the actual building itself as there is nothing round here really like it. It is so 1950's. Britain has got to be very careful that it does not lose its entire 1950 heritage.

I'm ambivalent about moving into a new market, that does not bother me one way or the other, but I do think that the city council should decide what they want to do with the building. If we do move I think a lot of people will miss this market".

Market
Time-lines

The World in 1958, the year the market was born.

Pope John XXIII the son of a poor Italian farmer was crowned 262nd pontiff of the Roman Catholic Church

The Bossa Nova was created in Rio de Janeiro, thanks to Joao Gilbert's recording of "Chega de Sudade".

The first Trans Atlantic passenger jetliner service begins with flights between London and New York on the new British Comet Jet.

Munich air disaster occurred on February 6th 1958 - 21 dead, including 7 Manchester United players

Angelo Giuseppe Roncalli better known as Pope John XXII

The Great Chinese Famine begins in 1958 and ending in 1961 causing the death of nearly 30 million through a combination of natural disasters and poor planning.

Elvis Presley is inducted into the Army.

Best Picture of 1958: The Bridge on the River Kwai

Born in November 1958: Jamie Lee Curtis (American actress)

UK Number One single in the charts as the Market opened: It's All In The Game- by Tommy Edwards

UK Number One album in the charts as the Market opened: South Pacific, the Original soundtrack

Average House Price: £2,390

At this time, you probably would have been a Teddy boy or girl, and be listening to rock n roll, and buying your Brylcreem from the market.

Top seller South Pacific, it included, Happy Talk and There is Nothing like A Dame.

The World in 1968, the market is ten years old

British Post office introduces First Class post

Dutch Elm Disease continues to increase with tens of thousands of trees now destroyed

Senator Robert Kennedy is assassinated at the Ambassador Hotel in Los Angeles

The Kray twins, arrested for the murders of George Cornell and Jack 'The Hat' McVitie, members of the London underworld

The border between Spain and Gibraltar is closed

The Beatles create Apple Records and record "Hey Jude" as the first single on the label

Best Picture of 1968: Oliver

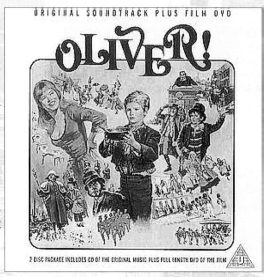

UK Number One single in the charts when the Market celebrated ten years: Sugar, Sugar by The Archies

UK Number One album in the charts when the Market celebrated ten years: The Hollies Greatest Hits by The Hollies

Average House Price: £4,344

At this time, you probably would have been a former mod just about getting used to being a psychedelic hippy, listening to Jimi Hendrix and The Beatles and buying your "I'm backing Britain" badge in the market, because it was 'Far Out Man', probably.

The World in 1978, the market is twenty years old

Black Market Clash

Britain launches the Motability scheme to provide cars for disabled people.

The Cult leader Jim Jones instructed 400 members of his church, "People's Temple", to commit suicide in Guyana.

Illinois Bell Company introduces first ever Cellular Mobile Phone System.

Argentina Wins 1978 World Cup in Argentina.

Best Picture of 1978: The Deer Hunter

First Test Tube Baby is born in England a girl Louise Brown, from in vitro fertilization

UK Number One single in the charts when the Market celebrated twenty years: Summer Nights by John Travolta/Olivia Newton-John

UK Number One album in the charts when the Market celebrated twenty years: Grease-Original soundtrack

Average House Price: £13.650

At this time, you probably would have been a punk rocker, listening to The Clash and The Pistols, screaming anarchy, bet you got your zips and safety pins in the market though.

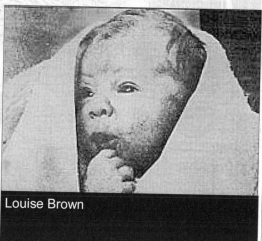

Louise Brown

The World in 1988, the market is thirty years old

The Hubble Space Telescope Goes into operation to explore deep space and is still in full use today mapping our universe

A bomb is exploded on Pan Am Flight 103 over Lockerbie in Scotland on December 21st

The English Pound Note ceases to be legal Tender

Widespread strikes in Poland by Solidarity Supporters

Stephen Hawking Publishes " A Brief History Of Time "

Best Picture of 1988: Rain Man

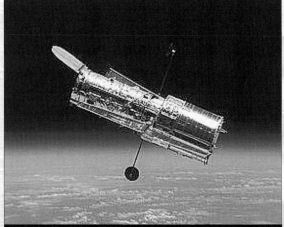

Hubble Space Telescope, scientists got to see the dark side of Coventry Market for the first time!

UK Number One single in the charts when the Market celebrated thirty years: Orinoco Flow by Enya

Money for Nothing

UK Number One album in the charts when the Market celebrated thirty years: Money For Nothing by Dire Straights

Average House Price: £61,020

At this time, you probably would have put down your Nintendo and unpacked that CD player you have been after for ages. Then it was on with Money For Nothing from Dire Straights, and out with the 'air guitar' wearing your denim jacket you purchased from the market.

The World in 1998, the market is forty years old

I cannot tell a lie-sorry wrong President.

After many years of troubles in Northern Ireland both sides agree to the Good Friday peace agreement

The splinter terrorist organisation "The Real IRA" plant massive car bomb in Omagh, Northern Ireland killing 27

France Wins 1998 World Cup in France

Viagra was released

The Search Engine Google is founded

The US President Bill Clinton denies he had "sexual relations" with former White House intern Monica Lewinsky, but later admits it

Best Picture of 1998: Shakespeare In Love

UK Number One single in the charts when the Market celebrated forty years: Believe by Cher

UK Number One album in the charts when the Market celebrated forty years: I've Been Expecting You by Robbie Williams.

Average House Price: £75.806

In 1998 you were probably wondering if you should upgrade to Windows 98, or buy a new Apple Mac. Blokes were definitely not looking in the market to buy a David Beckham-style sarong to wear however!

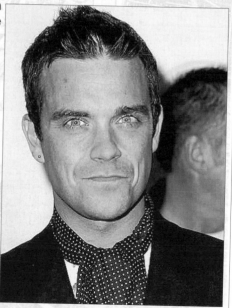

Robbie Williams, as expected.

The World in 2008, the market is fifty years old

Barack Obama is inaugurated to become the 44th President of the United States. He is the first African American to hold the office

Property prices continue to fall on both sides of the Atlantic in Europe and America causing hardship to many homeowners and problems for the financial institutions

President Bush signs the $700 billion bailout / Rescue package bill (Emergency Economic Stabilization Act of 2008)

Mr President

Spain finally ended their 44-year wait for a trophy when Fernando Torres' exquisite first-half goal gave them a deserved 1-0 victory over Germany in a fast and furious Euro 2008 football final

2008 was the International years of the Frog, the Potato and sanitation

Viva Espanya

Best Picture of 2008: No Country For Old Men

UK Number One single in the charts when the Market celebrated fifty years: Hero by the X factor Finalists

UK Number One album in the charts when the Market celebrated fifty years: Funhouse by Pink

Average House Price: £211,410

At this time, you probably would have been moaning about the pending credit crunch, listening to Duffy on your i pod and buying your vegetables in November at 1958 prices at the market

Traders
Memories

There was a young man– In his own words Michael Finnegan

If there's something going down in the market, chances are Market Operations Manager Michael Finnegan will be there, here's how the man himself sees it.

"I came over from Ireland to Coventry in 1961, when I was 16 years old and I worked as a tailor in Smithford Way for three months. The hours were long and the pay was no good. So I left and got a job in the market, working as a barrow boy for Ronald Johnson who had six stalls. Mr Johnson had a manager, a man by the name Ray Craddock and when he retired, I thought my chance to be a manager had come! Instead he brought in his ex-wife and daughter to run the stalls. I continued for about two years then decided to leave and after twenty years in the market, I got a job in a foundry in Baton Road along with my brothers. I only worked four days a week and on occasion myself and my wife Jean would go into the market and Mrs Johnson or her daughter would ask us to sort out the stalls or warehouse for stock checks. I ended up doing this on a regular basis.

After around two years the foundry closed down and I asked if there were any market jobs coming up and the Market Manager, Mr Harry Phipps, told me to bide my time for a couple of weeks. So, in the mean time I helped out on a couple of stalls (Mr Johnson's and Mr Morgan's). This is a period that always sticks in my mind, because it was during the English potato famine and we had to import German potatoes and they smelled awful!

The market was very busy in those days with all the factories close by, like the GEC and Rotherham's. Their staff would come in the morning and the stalls had to be ready by 7.30 to trade to them, they also came in during lunch time and when the had clocked-off. The market had a lot of characters, like Albert Norman, Albert Edwards, Tommy & Ina Morgan, Bobby Arthur (a boxer who had a fish stall) and a man who would take the boards off the stalls in the morning and put them back at night, his name was Harold.

In 1983 I got the job as a Market Attendant. Soon after I became Shop Steward. Twelve months later I got the job as Assistant Supervisor in the market office, eventually becoming Market Operations Manager".

Mick- the market is everything!

41

Neil Moran – I Remember it Well - His own words

"Tying in with two tone, back in 1969 I worked on Abingdon's stall as a Saturday boy. They sold Levi, Staypress, Brutus, Ben Sherman, Crombies and Harringtons. At lunch time the fruit and veg traders would go into the Market Tavern at 12 and come out about 3.30 much the worse for wear. One of the traders I used to work for was Lou Curaton who was the worse for wear one Saturday. Earlier that day another trader called Chick had had an altercation with a group of lads who came back later in the afternoon to sort Chick out. Lou decided he was going to go over and help him but the lads seeing the state he was in picked him up and sat him on the floor on his backside then picked up a melon and smashed it over his head. He was sat there, a melon on his head, it was one of the funniest sights I had ever seen in the mar-

Neil on the left, dressed as a Girl Guide.

ket. I wished I had a photo as it would have been really brilliant.

One joker stuck 2 foam blocks shaped like spurs on my dads heels. They were about a foot long and he walked around for about an hour without realising.

Another story, a group of lads came to Abingdon's stall being quite cheeky to Barry the Saturday lad and Barry gave them back as good as he got. Later on that day they returned with reinforcements ready to have a go. They hit Mark, another Saturday lad, across the head with a metal bar. They had got totally the wrong person! That must have been some surprise to him!.

There has always been characters in the market. Like the man they called 'Happy' always walking around with his sandwich board or Little Mary, a really nasty customer who would chase you round the stall and if the stall was shut she was so small that you couldn't see her over it, her language was absolutely blue.

I remember when somebody had some money taken out of the till and we all piled out after him and caught the thief in Argos and we got the money back. All of a sudden everybody seemed to have some money go missing from their tills.

Christmas Fancy dress 1987, below with Sky Blues legend Brian Kilcline, photos by Jean Gallagher

Jean (Gallager) The Knicker Queen

Frank and Jean

"Christmas Eve used to be the day that shop workers went to work in fancy dress. This also applied to the market stalls. In those days (when we were busy) I had 4 girls who worked for me and every year we dressed up. I remember one year in particular when we were all snowmen and got our photo in The Telegraph, quite a feat in those days. Brenda and Owen Moran were on the committee and they organised a fancy dress competition to be held on Christmas Eve and to be judged by several people including stars from the pantomime at the Belgrade and footballers from the city. Brenda and Owen worked very hard and got most stalls to participate. I racked my brains to try and think of something different for my girls and I and I came up with Pearly King and Queens. It took me 8 weeks to sew button on to skirts, jackets, waistcoats, hats and trousers. My husband, who at the time had a children's wear stall said he did not want to dress up. I tried to talk him into it, but he was adamant that his staff were not taking part. So I went on sewing buttons and recording cockney music to be played on my stall throughout the day. Christmas Eve was getting closer and most of the stalls in the market were going to dress up.

My costumes were finished I had 3 queens and a king, we looked great, or I thought we did. Pressure was put on all stalls to join in, the market wanted 100% support. Two days before the big day my husband decided they would dress up after all so I had to come up with a theme and the costumes in 48 hours. I dressed my husband as Count Dracula and the girls who worked for him as his brides. It was all done very quickly but they did look good. Christmas Eve came and every stall in the market had taken part. The atmosphere was terrific. The judges came round and the best stall chosen. The winner was a lady who worked for Marc Bates, she was a chicken. To my dismay my husband's stall came second in their hurriedly put together outfits and my stall whose costumes had taken me weeks to make only got 4th place It was the best Christmas Eve we had in the market. Dressing up fizzled out then mores the pity.

A life less ordinary

We think nothing of nipping into town to do a bit of shopping in the Market, but there are some people who's personal journey's have been less than easy, and look upon the Market as refuge to an alternative life that most of us in the west could not comprehend.

Mohammed Saeed like many Market Traders, is happy to have his stall in the Market, but Mohammed's reasons are probably very different to his fellow Traders. Born in Khost, Afghanistan, he once ran a very successful medical store in the town. Khost, is a large city situated on the East of the country close to the Pakistani border, it was besieged for five years during the Soviet War in the 1980's. In those days the Soviet Army used it's airfield as a helicopter base, now the American forces are stationed there. In the words of Mr.Saeed, "Afghanistan became a very difficult place to live because the Taliban were coming in every night to my city, I lost everything there".

When he came to Britain he settled in Birmingham where he worked in a Fish and Chip shop, "I wanted my own business again like I had in Khost", He said. "So I decided to start this fruit and veg stall in Coventry Market, and I now have two stalls and hope to have more. I have been here for 18 months now. I travel from Birmingham each day".

His new life is all very different to perpetual conflicts in his homeland, there are obvious sacrifices though, Mohammed's Mother still lives in Khost. "I miss my Mum", he said. "She still lives in Afghanistan , I went over to see her last year, but we had to meet up in the capital Karbul. You see everything is different over here I could not believe it when I saw a train for the first time, because Afghanistan has been at war for 40 years there is nothing left. I have never looked back since I came to Britain it is a very nice country everybody and everything in it. People in the Market are very friendly both Traders and Customers".

Mohammed's story is an inspirational one, he sought the safety of Britain and is now a successful businessman all over again "I came to Britain as a refugee", he smiled. I'm now a British Citizen".

Mohammed at his stall

45

Frank Gallagher – As I recall

I became a stall holder in Coventry Market in Oct 1973, having been made redun
dant from the Triumph Motor Cycle Engineering Co. I then proceeded to run m
small business for 31 years until my retirement in Oct 2004, having met som
very interesting characters and making many friends.

One such character I met from the start was Harold Robinson, a very scruffy an
smelly gent who would walk to the market from where he lived near Highfield R
in Stoke. He would arrive at the market early just before most traders and woul
do any odd job for a bob (a shilling in old money) but his main job would be t
take the boards off the stalls and put them back on after a day's trading. But wo
betide anyone that had upset him, he would bring the boards and throw them int
the storage cupboard coming very close to decapitating any passer-by. Althoug
a man of few words he would sometimes point to the sky ranting on about thos
"blinking monkeys", probably those traders who would have one joke to many wit
him.

Whether it was in the depths of winter or the hottest of summers his trademar
attire would always be the same heavy boots, 2 pairs of trousers, an old jacke
that many a dog probably slept on, a scarf knotted at his neck (I never did se
him without this) and his big flat cap. Yes, Harold was indeed a character nov
long gone.

In general most of the market traders in Coventry Market were a good humoure
relatively happy bunch although occasionally the odd disagreement did occu
usually when the traders had retired for a liquid lunch in the very popular Marke
Tavern. They would either skip back to the market after a great session or on oc
casions trading punches and shouting obscenities at one another.

Most of the traders had big hearts and on many occasions donned fancy dress t
raise money for very needy charities such as Snowball etc. We even had a go
society within the market which became allied with traders from other market
such as Northampton and Leicester. One of our better golfers who was very we
known in the market was Peter McGregor. He was disabled and confined to
wheelchair but by using and swinging with one arm in a specially adapted whee
chair actually became a British Paraplegic Golf Champion and in 1962 in Australi
won gold in table tennis.

1987 saw the market completely decked out in sky blue when every trader be
came a Sky Blue Supporter. None bigger than the Donnelly brothers, Pete an
Bernie, who for years have followed them through thick and thin. It is said the
have sky blue blood running through their veins although blood pressure ha
risen in the last few seasons".

Above Anne Marie and Tracie of Ben N Zaks Florist, and below Anwar and Ahmah of SD Fresh Fruit and Veg

47

Feels Like The 4th July

4th July formerly (American Imports Ltd) sell All American Foods, sweets, drinks, snacks, breakfast cereals and if it's American they hope to sell it. Here's their story in their own words.

"It all began with Lisa Hollins and Michelle Conway, two mums and friends both born on same day, 12th December, just a year apart. We had a dream to start up our own business but not really knowing what we wanted that to be. After we both discovered products from America and looking into importing the products back in January 2008, we thought two heads are better than one and "hey presto" American Imports was born. We first started trading out of Nuneaton Open Air Market (Saturdays only) in May 2008. We looked to expand as thing were going well. We

discovered Coventry Indoor Market. Which I did not know about (as Michelle is from Geordie Land). The Market Management staff have been great. We signed up to the 16 weeks business start up with 2 week rent free, this gave us the time and saved us money while setting things up. It is a retail outlet without the retail overheads. Starting Trading July 2008 and not looked back since. However it has not been without its ups and downs. What happens to me happens to Lisa and vice versa (must be the born on same day thing)".

Michelle (left) and Lisa (right) of 4th July

Terri Harman –Reflections

"I was a Saturday girl on Peggy Tweeds leather handbag stall from about 1979 - 1982. I was paid more than all my friends who worked very hard on the fruit and vegetable stalls, they had to stand on their feet all day and had dirty hands and chipped nails. Initially I was paid £4.00 plus 2 1/2 pence commission for every pound. My wages increased by increments of 50 pence but when Peggy realised that I was making anything up to £25 commission at Christmas time she stopped paying the commission and increased my wages to about £10 per Saturday.

Peggy was a very kind boss, unlike the bosses my friends had. She worked me hard but also gave me a good start in the world of business. She was trusting and gave me respect which bred loyalty. I still engage some of Peggy's work ethics in my working life today.

The friendship made whilst working the market were memorable and I have stayed in touch with some of the friends from the market. Lunch times were fantastic. We would all try to make sure we had our break at the same time and would head off to either Mario's cafe in Intershop (for a chip batch, lots of salt and vinegar) or the cafe on the market edge which was run by the family who still run the picture framing stall today. We would also sneak off for 'fag breaks' but we all agreed the worst part of the job was being sent down stairs to the underground store rooms. We pulled our empty trolleys through the crowds and entered the rickety old lifts. I always caught my breath as I pushed the gate together and pressed the down button. Would it work? Would the lift get stuck half way down? We didn't have mobiles in those days to call for rescue. The cold and smelly walk to the warehouse where I would have to bring up the bags which Peggy had sent me for and if I got the quantity wrong I would be in for a telling off. I would then have to make my way back to the store and ensure that my bounty did not fall of the trolley as I meandered through the crowds back to Peggy who would send me to wash my hands and make myself look respectable for the customers.

Near the end of the shift Peggy would let me rush to the butcher's stall and the fruit and vegetable stalls to buy the shopping at a reduced rate for my mum and dad. The stall holders would give me twice as much as I asked for and would charge me half as much. Liz Davey and her husband Jim were always particularly generous because I had worked for them for a short time and had helped them if they were short staffed on occasions.

The market tote would be called out by Eric Tweed who would ring his hand bell to get everyone's attention and the screams to reunite a missing child with their parents or guardians were legendary. We all looked forward to putting the boards on at night but it was a very skilful manoeuvre! Eric Tweed would do his rounds to make sure everyone had packed away properly and that all the young girls were safely out of the market before the lights went out.

Its lovely to walk through the market and see some of the old marketeers from the good old days, Neil's picture framing stall and his sister Nells Knickers and their parents jewellery stall were always an Aladdin's cave. I was often in trouble for not being able to pass those stalls without stopping. They were a very warm family who were proud of their stalls and their market community.

I often look back with a sense of pride that I was a Saturday girl at Coventry Market. It was a place that gave a lot of youngsters a start in life and a lot of parents pride in their children".

Say it With Flowers

Rob Lillis of Lillis Flowers fame told me of his roots (sorry). "My Mum and Dad had the stall before me, it was fruit and veg stall then. They were actually first in the market to bring in exotic fruit, they used to go over to Birmingham to buy yams and sweet potatoes before anyone else was selling them here. They were great days, I recall at Christmases everybody used to decorate their stalls with old spud and carrot bags, that was fun".

About twenty years ago, Rob changed from selling fruit and veg to flowers, I asked him what made him change? "To be honest fruit and veg was very hard work, getting up really early, we used to go to the Barras Heath Market, it was really busy in the old days. It's sad how it declined. My wife and I needed a change, it was much easier making a living selling flowers, I've been happy ever since and we have built up a good business".

Rob and Marie Lillis

Above Maurice,

Below– Jaynti,

51

Above, Pete Donnelly , John Harrison and Charlie present an Association cheque to the Lord & Lady Mayoress, Jack and Jill Harrison

Below, The Shoeking staff, Conor, Bill and Sophie

Joe from Maria's Bakery

"My mother and father in law set up the stall in 1977. My father in law didn't want to do it as he was an ice cream man at the time but my mother in law was adamant and it went from strength to strength for 14 years. My father in law had a serious accident and was forced to retire. I met Catrina a couple of months later and took over the running of the stall. This is my 15 year.

Jerome Smith and Vicky Blackwell

and took over the running of the stall. This is my 15th year. When I first came I was the younger generation but now I am the old school. We started with a single unit but as we got busier increased it to a double. We have lots of regulars and serve between 350 and 650 people per day depending on the day. Its a fun place to work with a lot of banter going on between the stall holders. I wouldn't have wanted to do anything else.

We make about 150 custom cakes per week. The weirdest ones we have been asked to do were a man's privates and a wedding cake for a couple who were getting married in Africa and wanted a safari cake in zebra style. Sometimes we can spend as many as five days on one cake as they are a work of art and priced accordingly. We make them all in our bakery in Stoke.

A couple of characters I remember in the market were old Ron who used to be there singing and dancing every morning as we were setting up the stalls. Another character was Jeff Cramp, an old shoe trader who came from Leicester. As you can imagine there was always banter about the football clubs.

One particular time I remember was when Coventry got to the quarter final and Leicester had been knocked out. My wife and I did the stall up with blue streamers and balloons and a banner which read Good Luck Sky Blues from the Cramp family. It was only meant as a joke but Jeff took it the wrong way at the time, I am sure he would have a good laugh about it now".

Above-Where's Bill ? Below, still can't find the corners?

CORPORATION OF THE CITY OF COVENTRY

MAIN CONTRACTOR
WILLIAM
MOSS
& SONS LTD
LONDON
LOUGHBOROUGH
LIVERPOOL

RETAIL MARKET

ARCHITECT
A.G. LING B.A. FRIBA. MTPI
CITY ARCHITECT & PLANNING OFFICER
BULL YARD COVENTRY

CONSULTANT ENGINEER

QUANTITY SURVEYORS

Bill Duffin-A Reflection

There was one fruit stall trader Bill Duffin was telling me about who sold bananas oranges and mushrooms which were all delicacies in those days. "They only worked 3 days then, so if the mushrooms did not sell on the Wednesday he would put them in brown paper bags and attempt to sell them on the Friday. He also put all his money in an identically brown paper bag (we know where this is going don't we). One week trade was absolutely fantastic and all the brown bags went, hang on a minute, you said all the brown bags went, Oh dear, one lucky punter, got more than a bag full of mushrooms, he got the stall holders takings too. Of course he returned it as soon as he saw that a mistake had been made, err-did he heck as like, the trader had a real Shiitake day that day.

In the old days market rules were very protective about what you could sell on your stall and you had to stick to exactly to your own type of goods. If you sold footwear that is all you could sell not belts of bags. One Trader who sold high-class menswear, things like Harringtons and Crombies, tried to introduce other items. Very feminine pink candlewick dressing gowns appeared on the back of his stall selling at 6/7d . The Market Manager told him that no way could he sell them as they were obviously ladies wear and another stall holder had the right to sell such an item, he replied, calm as you like, oh they are for men who are cross dressers.

Shortages on stalls were common in the old days especially on the fruit and veg and one lady Mrs Johnson had not had any oranges on her stall for months and months. Eventually a boat came in from South Africa and it was her turn for the allocation, loads of boxes of oranges appeared and everybody descended on her stall. Mrs Johnson began to get more and more panicky as the crowd grew bigger and bigger. In the end she let out a scream and said "I'm going home I'm going home I can't cope" and ran off home leaving her stall unattended I don't know

The legend that is Bill Duffin of Shoekings

what happened to all the oranges but I'm guessing that people just helped themselves. It's hard to imagine orange shortages nowadays of course. I suppose that's where we get the phrase of a blood orange for Christmas.

Talk about 'on your bike'. Some of the Fruit and Veg stall holders actually came from Leicester by bicycle. Can you believe that they rode to Coventry on their bikes stopping on the way to call at the Barras Wholesale Market to place their daily order and then carry on to ride to the market. Their order was then delivered to them. At the end of the day they would ride all the way back to Leicester again, now that's keen.

A jeweller from London who had a stall in the market, didn't believe in banks and used to keep his money in bags in the loft and one day he went to get some money (probably to count it) and found that the mice had chewed it to pieces (I hate them mices to pieces springs to mind).

Harold of plaque fame was paid 2/- by stall holders to put the boards up on their stalls at the end of the day and he would swing them about and not care if he hit anybody".

TRIBUTE TO HAROLD

IN MEMORY OF
HAROLD ROBINSON
A FRIEND
WELL LOVED BY ALL
THE COVENTRY
MARKET TRADERS
DIED AUGUST 10th 1990
AGED 63 YEARS
SADLY MISSED BUT
ALWAYS REMEMBERED

Above, Matt from Baguette Bakery

Below, Nana, from Universal Foods.

Above Ryan & Chris at Chris's Toyland and Fancy dress

Below Ute and Michelle at the Market Cafe

The Heritage Stall

Bill Duffin along with his wife Sophie (and Conor) can always be found at the Shoekings stall, whether its slippers or Doc Martens you require. Although knowledgeable about most things, it's medal and local history Bill excels at. If you want to know something, chances are Bill will have some idea (after this book goes out he'll have me to thank for queues of people at his stall, ignoring his footwear and just asking him random questions). For me Bill represents the market best of all, and along with others, has helped to raise it's profile not to mention his work on the Market Traders Association. Apart from his shoe stall, he also looks after the market's Heritage stall, I asked him to tell me more about this treasure trove of historic delights.

"We opened a Heritage Stall in the market, probably 7 years ago after numerous members of the public kept coming to us asking questions, things like, do we know anything about Standard Triumph, or Coventry watches and had we heard of Stevenograph. We decided there was enough items that the traders had or we had purchased that we could open a stall. So we decided in our own little way that we would try and create some history about Coventry.

Things like the ribbon weaving industry were a very important part of the history of Coventry. Fancy ribbons were high fashion in the 18th and 19th century. People would travel from all over Britain to buy Coventry ribbons. They trimmed their dresses, coats and bonnets. Then in the mid 1800's cheap French woven items came into the country and almost overnight the ribbon weaving industry was on its knees. Companies like Stevenograph and Cash's then changed from weaving ribbons to weaving things that we know today like Cash's bookmarks and silk pictures and they in their own right became very collectable. So we had a selection of these things on display. People would come and talk about them and tell us their dad worked in the factories and that again was some of Coventry's past.

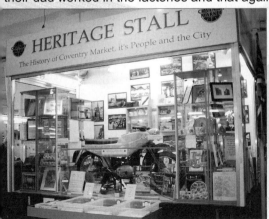

We also found there was an interest in the bicycle in Coventry's history, a very important part in its past life. The same with the watch making industry. Coventry was probably the world centre for watch making and in the 18th and 19th century some of the best watch makers in the world were centred in Coventry, and now no watches are made here".

A Dogs Day at Midnight for Paul Taylor

Midnight (don't call it Midnight Records, cus it ain't the name), is Paul Taylor to you and me, Coventry's only independent record and CD retailer. Having just celebrated it's 10th year in the Market, the stall is a breath of fresh air in the growing trend of the cult of the download.

"Couple of years ago when the Jailhouse venue in Coventry was open, I was having a perfectly normal day on my Midnight stall here in the market. I looked up and a couple of people came to my stall, they wore the hats and the coats and they looked like they were in a band. I didn't recognise them as such, I just guessed that it was a band playing at the Jailhouse that night. Looked up again and there was a bloke and a woman and it was Tyla from The Dogs D'amour. He was flicking through my CD's, through the cheap section, when he pulled a CD out and took it out of it's case, had a look at it and put it back in the case. Then he walked up to me and said, "Excuse me mate, this is the wrong CD in this case". I suddenly got it and said, "Yeah it's your CD isn't it".

It was a Dogs D'amour CD, first of all it was in the cheap section, secondly it was in the wrong case. To make matters worse, after I had apologised to him, he asked if I was coming to the gig at night, and I knew I was unable to make it, so I had to tell him no. I would have loved to have seen them, but he didn't seem to mind, and didn't bear a grudge. He signed a poster that I still have on the stall and I haven't seen him since".

Paul and that poster

Lindsey Joplin – All those years ago

Lindsey is one of those well known faces of the Market, one of those people I was told multiple times to "have a word with". Not surprising really, as he's been in the market since 1965, where he first worked for Cooper's glass and china.

"Cooper's also had stalls at the Hearsall Common Crock Fair when it came around and I used to serve on it. I used to go up the week before and help build the stalls. We met many people from all different parts of the country. Sadly over the years the fair just died out. We used to take a bloke called Harold up with us if we needed an extra pair of hands, we would sit him in the back of the van as he smelt like a polecat. Harold was famed for taking down and putting up the boards on the stalls. Actually before Harold I used to do it, I used to come in early and set up my stall then the women would shout me about 8.55 to come and take their boards down. It was first come first serve, so you can imagine it was quite a commotion, I think I got paid a shilling a stall. I did that from 1966-1972 then Harold took over.

We had all types in the market, Coventry City footballer David Cross coming in to buy dinner plates. I recall comedy stars Billy Dainty and Hattie Jacques from the Coventry Theatre Birthday Show came in, as did the manager of the Georgian State Dancers. He came down and ordered a dinner service, I delivered it by hand to the Theatre and I had to take it round to him. He ushered me in through the back door where there were ladies in various states of undress getting ready for the show, I didn't know where to look. He made me sit down in the front row and watch the show. I sat there for about five minutes then thought I had better

Lindsey -Then and now

61

In those days every stall opened Wednesday, Friday and Saturday. It was a bustling place on those days but on other days it was half empty. I eventually bought Arthur Cooper out in 1979. I paid £12,000 and he lent me half to buy the business. Cooper's were actually mentioned in a Coventry history book written by somebody in the Coventry Telegraph.

The glass and china trade was dropping off and by now the firms were opening shops at their own premises, so in 1984 I decided to change to selling carpets. There was a carpet stall in the market owned by a very mean man, he had 3 or 4 staff working for him but on a hot day he would walk past my stall with 2 ice creams eating both of them before he got back to his stall so he did not have to share them with his staff!! Frankie Addison was another trader who used to stand at the front of his stall smoking a big fat cigar he always had first class fruit and veg and woe betide anybody who touched it as he and his wife would have a big row with them.

An amazing find, The Flower sellers basket

Another character was a flower seller . She was a big lady. She used to have the flowers in a big basket which looked like a pram, she looked like a character out of a Dickens novel.

There were a lot of great characters who worked in the market, though how about this for one of the customer's antics. One day it was blowing a blizzard outside, snow all around, trade was dead and I had just decided to go home. Then this little old lady appeared carrying a teapot, we used to sell just teapot lids you see, and she had fought her way through the snow to get a lid for her teapot, I couldn't believe it!!".

**Above May of May's Fruit & Veg
Below Nigel from Randle's Clothes**

63

Above Dave and Bernie at The Market Heel Bar
Below Graham and Irena of Computer Corner

David Betts From Day One

Fruit and Veg man Dave Betts Senior has been at Coventry Market from day one. "I was selling pears while Princess Alexandra was on the podium, that was the first ever sale in the new market. I was 17, it was my dad and mums stall who came in the from Rex market. It was busy when it first opened, the river used to run along and I could see St John's church from my stall. But then it slumped as there was still a lot of building work going on. When the market started they were going to give the old traders a choice of which stall they wanted but at the 11th hour an argument broke out so in the end it was drawn out of the hat. Some people doubled up with empty stalls. After 12 months a lot of the old traders left but the market filled up and they actually had a waiting list at the Council.

At different times of the year we were very busy, like January to April we had the Canary King Edward potatoes in, they came in wooden boxes. I spent all Thursday afternoon opening the boxes which had wooden lids and were wired up as Friday was our busiest day. The stall holders had a lot of regular customers who stuck with them".

A real Market Dynasty– Mark, David Senior and David Junior
The Betts Boys

I asked David about some of the market characters, one very famous one, who crops up time and time again is Albert Norman. "Albert did painting he was on Midlands News and a member of the Royal Academy, said David, "I have two of his paintings During the war he and his wife had the only concession for pickled onions in Coventry and he became very wealthy. He had a telephone line put in down in the basement so that he could ring his bookie. He was a very benevolent man and would help anybody out in trouble. He even gave his stall to a lady. In the end he finished up very poor and the Market Federation helped him out".

There is one customer who will always be special to David. "I had one female customer come in and I told her I had nobody to help me on a Saturday so she said she would come in and just help me out just the once". She is still here 40 years on and what's more David ended up marrying the lady, and the whole family work in the market, a real market dynasty.

John Dixon-Pull Up An Orange Box

"One of the memories I have was the time my brother and I used to collect discarded wooden orange boxes and keep them in a shed behind our shop. Over 12 months, we would end up with a shed full of them (about 50). We would then sell them at 6d each to people who would be outside our shop when the Coventry Carnival was on, to sit on. After the event they would leave the boxes in the street, which we would then collect and spend the next few weeks chopping them up to sell as fire wood. This was our first encounter of being entre-preneurs. I was 8 and my brother was 11. Happy days!

I have since ended up setting up and running my own IT company, Computime IT Solutions Ltd for the last 25 years (merged in February with Acutec in Coleshill)".

No gripe with ripe tripe

August 21st 1999, was something of the passing of an era, in more ways than one. Hayes tripe stall closed for the very last time in Coventry Market. When I was growing up tripe was still being enjoyed by many people. I recall my Father eating this honeycombed white-stuff cooked in milk, even trying some myself, before knowing what it even was, let alone where it had come from (I doubt there is anyone reading this who doesn't know, but just in case, it's a cow's stomach lining). I remember the tripe shop on Ball Hill that became a tailors and eventually a cafe and that was only one of many places just in that area that sold this strange food-stuff.

George 'Tripey' Hayes began selling this 'delicacy' in Coventry in 1916, this man and the Hayes family were local tripe legends. The offal was originally brought to Coventry on the train from Manchester, until demand got so high that a shop was leased in Market Street and later a factory in Rowley's Green. During the First World War offal was rationed, until Mrs Hayes protested for three days at the Council House and she was given permission to sell off-ration! George 'Tripey' Hayes died in 1940 and the business changed hands many times, but the Hayes name remained.

Over the years of course tastes changed, the 'tripe generation' eventually all passed on and the demand for tripe passed with them. Can't see the kids of today eating 'tripe twizzlers' and 'tripeburgers'. As for me, I don't recall what it tasted like and to be honest I don't want to find out. It's inevitable that it would finally die out, but leaving aside the somewhat less than palatable aspect of tripe, its demise along with 'policeboxes' and pub 'outdoors' are now just nostalgic memories of a less hectic way of life we call the past.

Manageress Marie Harris (left) and her staff Madge Brown, Janet Rose and Sally Smith, prepare for the final day.
Photo Courtesy of the Coventry Telegraph

Who You Gonna Call......Paul Sadler.

Paul Sadler-behind you!

Paul Sadler is a well-known face around the market, as a long time Market Attendant, he has seen trends come and go. Indeed he was one of the first punk rockers of his day in 1979.

"In 1976 when punk came in I had a two foot spectrum Mohican" said Paul, "everyone was amazed, I was the face of punk to everyone in the market, the thing is everyone loved it, nobody said a bad word. I was an original punk and one of the very first two tone rude boys when that came in. I bought a lot of my gear from the market, tonic suits, Harrington's and Crombie's". He's not only seen trends come and go, but a few less 'earthly' things too.

"I worked nights and we used to hear footsteps in the early hours of the morning" Paul reveals, "sometimes we saw visions and heard voices. When we were all in the office we used to hear talking and rush out to see what was going on and there was no one to be seen. Before the market was changed we had two metal spiral staircases going to the basement and we would go to investigate and out of the corner of my eye I would see this dark shadow. We have definitely seen ghosts in here when we were working nights. There was one occasion when I was working on the shop floor in the market and my neck went cold and I knew a spirit had gone through me into the old fish market".

"My colleagues and myself all saw it usually between 1.30 – 3.30am in the morning" he continued, "in around 1983/84. The place was definitely haunted and we heard high heels and men's shoes and voices it was very scary at first but then you just got so that you accepted it. One man said to me did I really see that and I said yes this place is definitely haunted. I have always believed in the paranormal and ghosts".

So the next time you visit the market, just be aware, that the sound you are hearing may not all be of this earth, and that chill in the air may not be a loading bay door left open...spooky!

Smile with Daisy

One stall in the Market you are pretty much guaranteed to be greeted with a smile is at Daisy's Fine Foods, specialising in African and Caribbean produce. Daisy Oppon was born in Britain to a Dutch mother and an African father, who comes from a long line of businessmen. "That's probably where I get it from" smiled Daisy. "I worked in Marks & Spencer and I came into the Market one day, and it hit me that there was the need for an African/Caribbean stall, there was not one there, that was about six years ago. I just kept thinking about it, I was driving my husband crazy saying "why don't you get a stall in the Market as there is nothing out there and people are struggling." My husband said I should seriously think about it. At the time as I had a good job with Marks & Spencer, but kept wandering around the Market till finally I decided that this is it and I left.

"When I started it was not very easy" admits Daisy, My husband said "I told you so," so he took a three month holiday to help me set it all up. Setting up and getting stock meant I had to go to London every two days to get the fresh stock. I had no idea what it entailed and I had to get a few people to help me and tell me what to order, but after a few months I was okay, and I haven't been back to London in over two years now".

Silamo   Willkumm   Aloha mai   Oso oseyo

Daisy's Fine Foods has a strong international customer base; people from Brazil and Venezuela. Then you have Caribbean's, Africans, French and Europeans. They know what they want, like their spices and exotic vegetables. Over the years Daisy has learnt to stock just the right items, bringing her customers back every week. "It's a great stall, and I love doing it, you get to meet people and learn a lot every day. Your customers become your friends. When I started there was only me doing this, but now several African shops have opened, people try them but in the end they come back to us and they can get all they want on one stall with good quality and friendly service. With me I'm always thinking ahead but maybe I will come up with something in the future that is unique, but at the moment I am very happy here".

Eric Tweed man from the Fed

Eric Tweed was one of sixteen children from the largest family ever recorded in Coventry. He's also dedicated a lot of his life to the market trade, in many of its forms, including trader for 32 years.

"I worked in the wholesale fruit and veg Market and saw all the lorries filling up to go to the main Market and realized that is where I should be" said Eric."I thought I should try and get a business and go there, but as it worked out there was a bomb site in Hale Street near the old Opera House and the chap who was running it was giving it up, so I took that on and saved every penny I could and finally bought a fruit and veg stall in Coventry Market. In the mid 60's. I also bought a handbag stall for my three daughters as they didn't like the heavy lifting involved in fruit and veg".

Eric Tweed

His association with Federation began with his friendship with fellow stall-holder Arthur Frith. "Arthur sold curtain material on the Market" Eric said, "and he was the National President of the Market Traders Federation and asked me to accompany him to a meeting in Wales, and as his guest to the National Conference in Blackpool so I thought that would be good, a three day all expenses paid trip. From then on I began to become interested in the work of the Federation". "In the mid 80's there was only one person going for the Junior President's position, so they asked me to stand against him, so it was not a fait accompli, but amazingly I was voted in, and he wasn't". Eric also worked for the Federation as their Mobile Officer in a custom Winnebago, "I suggested they had a mobile home all decked out and to take it round the country to all the different Markets to explain our work to them, "reveals Eric. "They not only liked my idea, but asked me to run it. It worked really well and I was signing up 10 people a day to the Federation".

"When I was at the Fed I suggested we had MP's to represent the Market Industry. We had four MP's and one Lord. Lord Graham and I became good friends and I used to go to his house. In 1987 when Coventry got to the Cup Final I couldn't get a ticket at any price. He was kind enough to send me a couple. He was actually Lord Graham of Edmonton which was Tottenham. So on the day I travelled down first class bedecked in my sky blue hat and scarf. I showed my ticket to the Steward who said I was in the wrong side and to go across to the other side of the pitch which turned out to be the Tottenham end and I sat with all the Spurs wives and celebrities in my sky blue". Eric obviously got out unscathed, because he's still working for the Federation, and loving every moment of it.

I've always been keen to use the centre circle of the market to bring in things that you just wouldn't expect to see. We've had celebrity cookery and fashion demonstrations, Irish and Bhangra dancing, creepy crawly zoos where you could stroke a tarantula, bird of prey displays and our own Coventry Markets Got Talent, string quartets, tea dances and prize bingo, remote control car racing and football competitions just to name a few. The first display we brought in was Coventry farm. They came in for a week to show off the new born lambs, pigs, chickens, ducks, rabbits etc. I didn't expect to have to herd sheep and pigs through a busy Monday morning market to their pens, something that surprised even hardened market customers. We had to do that twice a day and the stress it was causing the managers let alone the animals I thought they would be happier to be fenced in overnight. A call at 5.00am the next morning from the Market staff described ducks flying across the market and rabbits and chickens wandering around the stalls. All I remember saying is "round them up then" putting the phone down and going back to bed .

If that wasn't bad enough Fifi and Bumble caused a riot when 1000's of children came into the market to see the TV stars. A queue went round the market twice whilst waiting for a photo, Bart Simpson caused more trouble when he totally forgot to come in for a visit. but we've made up for it with some lovely visits from Bob the Builder, the Snowman, Peppa Pig, Dora the Explora, Chitty Chitty Bang Bang, Noddy, Big Ears, Tessa Bear and Paddington Bear.

Before the roundabout was recited in the centre the area was also changed each year into a magical Christmas grotto with woodland walks leading to Father Christmas's snow chalet, 100s of trees and wooded bark pathways led past fairy ponds and wishing wells with snow falling on to the best grotto in the Midlands.

Something's are still just beyond our control. Some of the more memorable are the shy street magician who literally disappeared when the public approached him, the stilt walker whose first two steps led him to fall head first into the café and the living statue with the dubiously placed fig leaf.

But all these things could just not happen without the support and enthusiasm of the Market Attendants and Managers. These guys carry out all the work behind the scenes, changing the two ton skips with four wheel steer tractors, maintaining the Market, the rubbish compactors, going up in 20 foot scissor lifts to change light bulbs, recycling tons of cardboard a week and helping traders and customers make a continued success of the Market.

My hat goes off to these guys who come in a 5.00am every morning and those who scrub the floors through the night. These are the guys who are here now or have left in the last 13 years.

My thanks go to..........

Paul Sadler, Don Valentine, Robert Millichip, Roy Jennings
John Quigley, Alan Phelps, Chris Barsons, William Guest, Cliff Willis
David Cox, Dennis Ray, Harry Palmer, Lenny Percival, Cornelius Morris
Cliff Cranston, Tommy Hardiman , Mick Kelleher, Robert Pearson, Vince Gernon

And in the office, Eileen Scallan, Nima Jagatia, Georgette Stutins,

The Managers. Mick Finnegan and Chris Taylor.

Whenever you are in the city it's always worth a look to see what's going on, you
might be surprised.

Thanks Brian Sexton

Some of the team that keep the Market running - (L to R) Robert Millichip, Alan Phelps, Georgette Stutins, Chris Taylor, John Quigley, Don Valentine, and Mick Finnegan.

Fishy
Tales

The Life and Times of Rupert The Fish-The Codfather.

When I began doing 'market research' for this book one man's name kept cropping up, everyone told me to talk to Rupert. "He's the man who knows more than anyone" they said. For it's true, Robert Stevenson- AKA- Rupert the Fish-AKA– The Codfather is the undisputed 'knowledge' when it comes to Coventry Market. Despite now leaving his spiritual home at the market, Rupert is still a busy man, so I am indebted to him for allowing me to use HIS words on these next few pages.....Rupert it's over to you!

"Well where do you begin? In its origins Southall's fishmongers started way back in about 1911 when the family moved to Coventry. They set up in business in the city centre originally selling second hand house hold furniture, but according to family history, we soon saw an opening for a fresh fish merchant and Southall's fishmongers was born. We traded in various markets around Coventry relocating to the present market in 1958 , where I spent all of my spare time as I grew up, learning the ways of market life and finally settling into my own pitch when in 1991 my uncle retired and I took over his stall. Well what an eye opener to life that was, its one thing helping on the family stall, but suddenly running your own, well its completely different, getting up at 4am, off to the wholesale in Birmingham, then

then go to Coventry wholesale, then down to the market and open up for trading.

It was a busy life, selecting the best fish for the day, watching the weather, too hot too wet, too cold and trying to balance the buying to suit and of course there's the doldrums months of summer when everyone's off on holiday, but it was a good life and one I never regret leading. I think the pleasure of market life is its variation and the people you meet along the way, chatting to your regulars, meeting new one off customers and the hustle and bustle of market life makes for a varied and interesting life.

Market life has many spin offs and part of selling fish is supporting the people who bring it for you, namely the lifeboat crews and the fishermen via the Royal National Mission To Deep Sea Fishermen, We in the market always appreciated the sacrifices made by these people to catch and land our fish, so in return we held events to support then in return, fish filleting displays, charity auctions, carnival processions and of course the every present old faithful collecting boxes at each end of the fish market

Over the years we have raised many thousands of pounds to help both these great charities and in recognition of this fundraising, I was invited twice to the House of Commons to receive awards on behalf of the fish market, but as I have always said, also on behalf of the people of Coventry who donated their money to these two charities".

A proud Rupert and Lifeboat

now let me tell you a story ....or two about market events. Are you sitting comfortably , then I shall begin...

"Now when the brand new fish market in its present location was opened we had to have all new fridges and freezers, not a big deal you say, but it was a marked difference from our old freezers that were basically commercial uprights like in your house, to a big walk in freezer with metal floors and metal internal boxes to put the goods in. Well, no one told me your boots needed to be bone dry before entering the freezer, two seconds later I'm stuck to the floor like a fly on glue paper, okay I thought, no big deal, I'll just bend down get the stuff I need for the customer and pass it out to my waiting mate then free myself, oops, as I bent down my ear touched the metal box at minus 19c ,my ear instantly stuck to the box, ouch I said, or words to that effect, and called to my mate to help me as it began to hurt.

So there I was stuck by boots and ear to a walk in freezer, so like a real work colleague would, he dashed for help, NO! He dashed around the market looking for a camera and told everyone to come and see, there was I, stuck for 5 minutes with everyone howling in laughter at me, before someone got some warm water to free my ear and boots, I ended up with a large pad on my ear as it went nice and black later, the only consolation was they could not find a camera in time. Some mate, I later suggested to him that maybe his parents might not have been married!

Working in the market, you see many people come and go over the years, traders, customers, family and friends, we all pass on in the end. It was always a great sadness when your old regulars turned up no more, you knew Mrs and Mr 'X' would turn up at 10am every Tuesday for their fish and a chat and that next week only one person would come in. We sat and chatted and often passes a tear together, they were not just customers like in a supermarket. These were my friends and in some ways you felt like they were family, many customers had been coming to the family stall and market before I was born, they had watched me grow up as a little boy, been there as my friends and eventually chose to shop with me as my customers even bringing their own children to see and shop with me, but all over those years that friendship remained and I was always sad and upset when I learnt another of my regulars has gone.

Indeed the market was a great big family. Ok, you were in competition against each other and like in life, we had ups and downs and fall outs but we always made things up eventually as you realise life is about being a family and that's what the market was a great big family. Ii remember well times like when your fridge broke down, or when I got run over, hit by lightning and or family member was taken ill, who came straight round to help you, look after your stall and even lend you their staff to keep an eye on, your other market trader friends.

I also remember well, the day I fell and broke my shoulder in two places. I was on my own and fell. I woke up on the floor in agony, all I could do was shout for help, in seconds my colleagues from around my stall were there. Clive sorted me out, called an ambulance and took care of things , Dave sorted my customers and till, and many others all piled in to run the stall, make sure every thing was safe and to look after me as the ambulance took me away. Now that's what a real family of friends is, they all lost customers as they looked after me, but that did not matter to them. I needed some help and they willingly gave it. You might think this is stupid or even sad, but I always felt I owed the market and in particular my stall something for giving me a living and family business for 98 years, so every New Year's Eve I toasted the stall with a wee dram and said thank you to it for another years trade and to say goodbye to all my old lost customers and to welcome the new lives my younger customers would bring in to see us. I know its silly but I felt I wanted to.

On the day I closed down for good, as I shed a big tear, I patted the old girl on the door as I turned the key for the last time and said a big thank you to the market for the life and living it had provided me with, its been a good building and I hope it out lasts me for a long time to come yet. Well, as Rupert the fish, I was invited by a local commercial radio station to attend the Town and Country show and do a display of shellfish and play a taste it game live on stage. Live on stage the presenter of the breakfast show dared me to do a bungee jump with him, well what could you say, I could not back out in front of all those people, so off with a roving mike to the bungee jump area. Now to say I was a bit scared is an understatement, but then I thought it's all good publicity for the market. So as they strapped me up the bloke said, "you'll bounce well, we can put light ropes on you as your so small", a real confidence builder .

So up we went and as I opened my eyes and looked over the royal show ground I froze stiffer than a prawn in my freezer. I was petrified and it was only a 160ft jump. "Jump", I said no way, I couldn't even feel my legs, so like a real mate the presenter said "I'll help you, just hold the braces like instructed and I'll gently help you to the side". So they opened the safety gate and this big size 10 boot hit my backside and pushed hard, yes I was air borne and going down at a rapid rate of knots towards earth, as the ground came rushing to meet me I thought of all the things I should have done in life, was this the end? Did they connect the cable to the crane? Then I remembered it was going to be great publicity for the market, as I was then catapulted back towards the crane basket I could see the presenter frantically speaking into the portable microphone, so I knew it would be played for weeks on air, so as I shot past the cage and then dropped ground-wards again I thought of the market and the fantastic publicity it would bring! Eventually after six or so bungies up and down I came to a stop, was lowered to the ground and was freed from the harness. I was very shakily asked, did it all come out Ok? Well there was this very long silent pause and a sheepish look from said presenter.

Well I said, what's the audio like? Err, Err was the reply, someone forgot to turn the mike switch on. Some market publicity, so Nick Tuff Radio star somewhere , if you ever read this thanks a lot mate and I still hate bungies. The market was and is still full of characters, in all their different ways these people are what make a vibrant market .

As a child growing up in the market I can clearly remember people like Old Pem the flower seller , a big lady who liked a tipple in the old bird cage pub, she always had a cheery smile and a pleasant word. Then there was Albert Norman, a fruit and veg seller who also sold paintings on his stall, he would trade all day then go home to a row of cottages by the river Sherbourne and do a couple of paintings to sell the next day. Then there was the outside traders, the pitchers who travelled from London

Albert Norman, trader and artist

and stayed in local hotels in the week whilst they traded at the market. They had the pitch and patter to draw a large crowd and their stalls were always busy with jostling crowds around them, all looking for that bargain. In those days that certainly drew in the people, it was more like a stage show than selling a few towels , people came just to stand and listen and to be entertained, but usually ended up buying something as they were swept along with the flow.

Every generation in the market has its own characters and in my time there were many who I fondly remember, like Ted Pindar, Gerry Dunn and many others in the old fish market, who were always there for you and lent a guiding hand to the younger ones. Saturday night was the pitching time in the market and these men certainly knew how to Knock Out on a Saturday evening, their pitch and banter was a real fun event but it really sold the fish too.

I'm sure that as the market progresses into the 21 century and when we are all long gone, we too might be remembered as market characters, but there will be others to replace us, exciting eccentric and one offs to be the new characters of Coventry market.

Ok so I had a fun side too and enjoyed being on the radio as Rupert the Fish, I saw it as giving something back to my customers, a bit of fun, with a serious side too. I always felt if I could make someone smile and laugh then I'd had a good day, ok, not everyone enjoyed my style and people came and told me so , but you can't please everyone can you? I do hope that I did achieve something and made Coventry a better happier place to live in. I know we have lots of smashing people in Coventry who listened to local radio or read the Telegraph, as every Christmas for over 15 years we helped in the annual toy appeal and the Coventry open Christmas shelter appeal. People used to come and give toys and food to both of these charities at my fish stall, even in the depth of recession, people gave what they could afford, but as I always said it did not matter how much, or big or small the gift was, it was given with love to someone we never knew, which made us all Coventry's own secret Santas.

Rupert and Bob Brolly, well I couldn't do a book and not include me mate Bob in it.

Well unfortunately , things have to end and in 2008, I saw the present recession coming and reluctantly decided after nearly 98 family years in the market to call it a day. My customers were getting fewer as they grew older and passed away and the younger ones went to super markets for their food shopping. I hung up my apron and rested my wellies for the last time on May 10th 2008 and on the Monday morning started my new life as a gardener / grounds man. That too has limitation due to the winter and I was offered a job in a store warehouse with some gardening in summer. I'm happy, I work with a nice bunch of lads the works different and interesting and as they do say, variety is the spice of life".

Kath Southall (Rupert's Mum) first fishmonger to sell continental fish in
Coventry fish market Circa 1970

Clive Miller – Fishmonger

"My family have been fishmongers for the last 230 years, and I have been in the market for 15 years.

We get all kinds of people come to the stall, from the very rich to the very poor, from the Right Honourable to some poor people like refugees who have just come to Coventry that month. The richer people buy Dover sole, halibut, wild sea trout and wild salmon and will buy fish for barbeques like herring, sardines or mackerel. At the other end of the scale they buy herrings, sardines and salmon heads and

Clive knows his plaice

bones, they are all in the queue one after another. This only works in the market as both sectors cannot buy what they get from us in a supermarket. If you want to impress your friends at a dinner party you need to go for something that is really niche and unique. They know that they cannot get that anywhere else like wild sea bass, sea trout and salmon.

The big trend is not the switch from salmon now being cheaper than cod but the switch from which ethnic minorities are coming. Now we sell loads of Tilapia where we once sold very little. When the Polish come we now sell lots of carp, people from Cameroon like to buy Troika so the market has to react quickly to meet all their needs. We sell Trevally for people from Northern Sri Lanka and we also have customers from the Caribbean and Brazil. People from Iran and Iraq the Northern water people or marsh Arabs want fresh bream and carp. All these things are really noticeable and you can tell exactly what ethnic groupings are coming to Coventry, by what fish they are actually purchasing.

Some of my more vivid memories are of the 40th anniversary and the 50th Anniversary (I was Chairman of the Market Traders Federation on the 40th Anniversary) and the coming back of the roundabout. Also the nightmare we had when the redevelopment was being done when the thermal insulation would not stick. Some friends from the past were Robert Stevenson on the fish stall and his brother Roger who was an artist on the shell fish stall, they were very charismatic. And Mr Cramp on the shoe stall we all used to have a good laugh, we still do but it is mainly with our customers now".

Some Fishy Tales from Fishy Clive

"One Christmas down the old market when my parents were still working, I was in charge of buying all the turkeys, geese and ducks. Two days before Christmas It was obvious that I had bought too many, I was not happy. I never swore in front of my mum ever, but I forgot myself and regretfully, I did that day. She just slapped me round the ear hole. I was 38 years of age and it was in front of all my staff and customers. I went as red as a beetroot. It just goes to prove that you are never to old for a slap!

Then there was the time I bought some live eels. They are slippery fellows and get everywhere, so my third wife Mandy was wearing elastic bands round the bottom of her trousers to stop them going up her legs. We counted ten of them when we started but by the end of the day we only had nine of them! We later found the missing eel in a bucket of water in the back of the stall.

Fishy Clive and not an eel in sight

John Twite on the fruit and veg stall used to ring a bell when a child was lost and if a shoplifter was about he used to ring it and shout "thief in the Market", to warn everybody. One day this bloke picked up a bag of pickled onions off his stall and walked off with them. John followed him all the way to Pool Meadow and asked him if he wanted to pay for them or do you want to take them back. He told the thief, "I saw you steal them and I have policeman behind me". So the thief said he would pay for them but John made him take them all the way back to the stall and then told him he didn't want his type of customer again.

Russ Fisher had a stall in the middle of the market one Christmas he had hundreds of Christmas trees all round his stall. It was crazy, they were on it and behind it, all over the place. There was a bloke called Tony Price who had a French horn so we decided to have a hunt through the trees, so he blew the horn and about five of us including Adrian Foster who was known as the mad butcher went through the trees. Adrian had secreted a hare under his coat and Russ Fisher was going mad about us all going through his trees when Adrian came out with the hare and put his finger under its chin, moving it and stroked it pretending that it was alive. He then pretended that it had bit him so he walloped it across its neck. On old lady had witnessed all this, and began shouting that they were going to report him to the RSPCA, for animal cruelty!

For my first days wages when I was 10 years old I did everything my Dad has asked me to do clean down, scrub down anything he wanted. I started at 5.30am and finished at 5.00pm I thought I was going to get at least four shillings (20p today) for I had worked really hard. At the end of the day my Dad gave me a spanking new 10 shilling note. I felt like a millionaire".

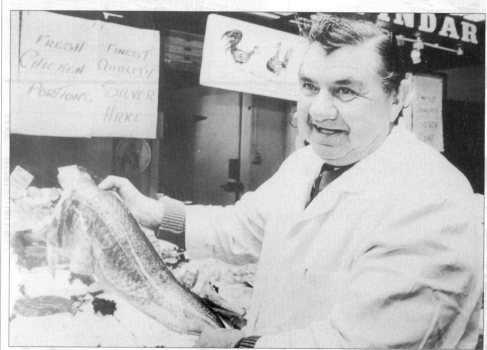

Above Fishy Ted, Father of Fishy Clive

Left Clive in his younger days at the fish market.

Ron Farmer, the other type of fish related stall in the market

A busy day at the fish market

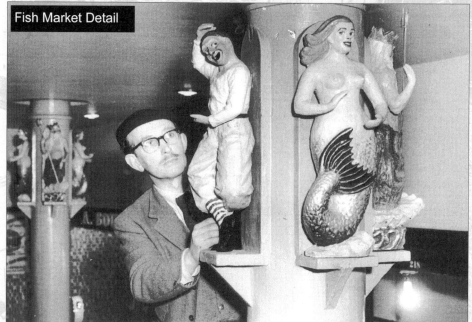

Fish Market Detail

Round and Around

The Roundabout

On discussing the planning of this book the one aspect of Coventry Market that was mentioned to me the most was the roundabout, everyone seems to have at least one memory of this well loved focal-point. It's even been immortalised in song by Crokodile Tears.

I recall going on it myself as a small child (obviously). It was just something about the fact it was in its own little area with the café hatch and benches all around. A oasis of calm far away from the hustle of the market floor. Well that's the poetic view of it, when the kids were set loose there was no quiet haven. The bells rang for the umpteenth time and the screams of delight mixed with the tears from the children that were never quite sure about the whole thing (sorry, but I steered to the right and it went left, I steered to the left and it went right, what's a young chap supposed to do?)

The famous roundabout, was originally owned by 'Uncle Jack' and Flora Statham they acquired their first roundabout in 1946, parking it on bomb sites after the war moving on when the land was redeveloped. In these days Flora and Jack lived in a single-decker bus parked next to wherever the roundabout happened to be. They eventually moved to The Rex and later the Barracks Market. In 1958 the famous roundabout was moved to the brand new 'Round' Market, and history was made for Flora and Jack when their roundabout became the first one ever officially opened by Royalty, Her Royal Highness Princess Alexandra on 4th November.

An early shot of the Roundabout from above

Jack was born in Spon Street and was an electrician before the war, serving his apprenticeship at The Daimler later moving to The Humber. After marrying Flora, he decided to leave factory life and he bought a roundabout and travelled the fairs. A Councillor had seen Jack at a GEC fete and asked

How sad is this picture? The Market Roundabout is dismantled. The good news was.... it would return.

him to site his merry-go-round in the city centre just for a few days, it was so successful Jack was asked to stay.

As this book was nearing completion, we heard of the sad death of Flora Statham who died aged 97. Flora was the daughter of a travelling showman and the devoted wife of Jack. Flora's nephew Anthony Stokes who now runs the Roundabout in Coventry Market with his daughter Rachel, said of his Aunt Flora, "Flora loved kids, and she loved the roundabout. In those days people used to leave their kids on the ride whilst they went and did their shopping. They knew they would be safe and looked after with Flora and Jack."

The fame of the Market Roundabout was brought home to Flora when she was on holiday in New York, whilst eating dinner at a Manhattan restaurant she was interrupted when someone approached her and declared, are you the lady from the Coventry Market Roundabout? Obviously her fame had got 'around'.

Jack and Flora
Photograph courtesy of The Coventry Telegraph

When I asked about the roundabout people talked of ringing the bell and the clattering sound the whole thing made. I laughed when one lady told me that she used to put her child on the ride and go off and do her shopping in the market. After mentioning this to a few people I soon realised it was common practice, not something you could get away with so easily in modern day society I would assume.

The roundabout did its job for 42 years, then when the area was redeveloped, it had to go. As expected there was a public outcry, but it's time had come, and in 2000 it closed down. That of course was not the end of it of course, some suggested that it's absence was affecting footfall in the market and the cries of "Bring Back The Roundabout", got increasingly louder and louder. Enough to prompt Coventry City Council into bringing it back. An outside location was no longer an option, so it was given pride of place in the very heart of the market, right in the middle (covering the historic mosaic, though I don't recall any outcry about that, I assume it would have rattled somebody's cage).

In October 2003, it returned, with a big opening with the then Lord Mayor Sucha Singh Bains doing the honours with children's favourite Noddy present to add even more to the childhood nostalgia. The ride was fitted with new mechanics, but all the original features were restored and reused. The first week it was free (with the first 100 children all receiving a free gift) then 50p a ride after that.

As it is today with Anthony and Rachael Stokes

THE STOKES FAMILY ARE VERY SAD TO ANNOUNCE THAT AFTER 54 YEARS IN COVENTRY THE CHILDREN'S ROUNDABOUT WILL BE CLOSING FOREVER ON SATURDAY 3RD JUNE DUE TO THE MARKET DEVELPMENT. WE WOULD LIKE TO TAKE THIS OPPORTUNITY TO THANK ALL OUR CUSTOMERS PAST AND PRESENT FOR ALL THE GOOD TIMES.

THE ROUNDABOUT CAFE

Here's Chris's memories of the Market and that Roundabout!

I grew up like generations of Coventry school-kids, enjoying a treat of a ride on Coventry market roundabout as a reward at the end of a well behaved shopping trip (perhaps not every time though!) Sometimes we might even have a bag of chips from the café there and sit eating them on the low wall, while our parents gossiped and drank tea in the seated area. Yes, we'd suffer lots of "Birdie Songs" by the Tweets, but every now and then there would be a gem played such as Thunderclap Newman's "Something In the Air" and it seemed like we could fly like birds around that merry-go-round when they came on. The proprietor of Statham's Roundabout, Jack Statham, always seemed to look sad to me, totally at odds with the jolly children's faces that spun around him.

I have family connections with 'Uncle Jack Statham's merry-go-round by the way. My grandfather, Sidney, designed and made the steel shutters for the ride which went up last thing every night. When I heard about the merry-go-round's closure, I was saddened to think of the children that would miss out on something that I'd so enjoyed at their age. This inspired me to write a song about the merry-go-round for my band Crokodile Tears called "Remember the Sound (of The Merry-go-round)". We also pressed up save the Roundabout badges and spoke to the local press about this campaign when we released the record.

They of course finally re-located the ride in the middle of the market but it's not the same and the music (in my opinion), is not as good as it was, but that's just me getting old though my grandchildren don't seem bothered about going on the ride much these days and that's not due to musical differences!

Now it's happening again, and the merry-go-round, is under threat and needs saving. Only this time it's worse, because the lunatics not only want to get rid of the merry-go-round, but also the circular market (revolutionary in this country at least) that surrounds it. This time I have to admit that I'm not so much concerned about the roundabout itself, but about the loss of the market itself along with the community that work there.

When the Roundabout's future looked grim, there was one guy who was prepared to fight the decision. That guy was (and still is in fact) Chris Sidwell, musician, teacher would-be politician and general all round nice guy. In 1999, he and his band Crocodile Tears (or Crokodile, depending his mood) released the CD "Merry -go-round EP". The lead track being "Remember The Sound (Of The Merry-Go-Round)".
Here's the lyrics to the song, words & music Christopher Sidwell 2009.

Remember The Sound (Of the Merry-Go-Round).

The boys go up and down
Around the old man in the centre of the merry-go-round
Their shouts and screams have filled his dreams
Seeing them bound up onto the merry-go-round

Is the old man sad successors been found
Now he's come to the end of his ride
On the merry-go-round

The Mums and Dads gave their last pound
To the old man in the centre of the merry-go-round
Came to the market when they were kids
Still remember the sound of the merry-go-round

On white horses they'll be taking him
One last ride around the merry-go-round
Is the old man sad successors been found
Now he's come to the end of his ride
On the merry-go-round

Below– CD cover, Mr Sidwell and Official Crocodile Tears campaign badge

Customers
Memories

Customers' Reflections

As a child in the early 60s, I remember a stall that had a bell that was rung by hand. If a child got separated from it's parents, the child would be taken to this stall and the bell would be rung to let the parents know where they were. I remember it well because I got separated from my mother on several occasions. I also have fond memories of the roundabout outside the market because my mother couldn't get me off it while the Beatles records were being played. **John Shields**

When I was about 9 or 10 years old I used to go through the market on the way to my Gran's. I used to buy an ice-cream from Victor the Italian ice-cream man and then would stand outside the market to watch Lou auctioning items off, I found it very exciting. His stall was at the back of the market and he sold textiles and anything else that he could get his hands on. I remember his catch phrase was "Give us a shilling" he seemed to charge a shilling for everything. **Faith Parker**

Years ago there used to be lots of people in the market, I used to be very frightened of all these people rushing around. Some were even on bikes. I think the market has gone down as there used to be a stall that sold spare parts for Dinky toys, where you could always buy the tyres and lots of material stalls, now there is only one. I suppose in those days lots more people used to sew and knit. Now I like to look at the Asian sari stall they are always so colourful. **Wendy Ingram**

One of the characters of Coventry Market for Maurice Burnell, was Dave Harvey.

Maurice Burnell

"He was a great friend of mine" revealed Maurice, "He ran the DIY stall, it was like an Aladdin's cave. If he didn't have want you wanted in stock, he would make sure he would get it in for you. When Dave's wife Jill passed away with cancer, the market traders did a sponsored walk and raised £980. I put in £20 to round it up to £1000. On occasion I would mind his stall for him. He came back one day and I told him eagerly that I had made a sale or two, he said 'Wow!' So before he got too excited I explained the sales were for just 50 Pence. He just said 'nice' exactly like Onslow in Keeping Up Appearances and we just rolled about laughing. Dave also died of cancer and before his death he told me that he had some lovely memories of the people in the market, he is remembered with strong affection." **Maurice Burnell**

Looking back with Wyn Taylor

Wyn is a lovely lady who came to see us in the Market Parlour, during our thirst for market knowledge. Wyn now 84, began working with her sister Joy Chamley at the old Rex Market, moving into the new market when it opened in 1958. They worked for Jack Turnock, a Potteries man who had several china stalls in various Midland's markets. Another one of Wyn's sisters, Norah French also worked on the stall.

"We normally worked on Wednesday, Friday and Saturday for Jack" said Wyn, "Jack eventually retired and my sister Joy bought the stall from him. We all continued to work there until 1985, when Joy retired and we all followed suit." She continues, "I recall that it was a long day standing behind the stall and the most tiring job was opening up in the morning, taking all the shutters off and getting the china out and arranging it. This of course was done in reverse again at closing time. It was quite often six before we finished, and the part-time wages in those days was not like they are today."

"I did get to meet a lot of interesting people" admits Wyn, "including the sister-in-law of film star Alice Faye. I told her how much I admired Alice and her husband Phil and when she returned to Hollywood she arranged for Alice to send me a signed photograph of herself and one of her husband Phil Harris. They also sent me a record of Phil's greatest hits including "The Dark Town Poker Club" and "Woodman Spare This That Tree.""

"I still shop in the market, mainly using the vegetable stalls, there are many of the old traders still active there."

Above Wyn holding a picture of herself and her two sisters on their china stall and above, that signed photo from Hollywood star Alice Faye.

Roger and Julie Griffith at the benches by the roundabout

Looking back with Roger Griffith.

"I used to live in the city centre" said Roger, "My wife Julie and I used to own a guest house for 13 years. It was originally called The Victoria but we changed it to the Abigail as we wanted to be at the beginning of the alphabet in the phone book. So we spent a lot of time in Coventry market and still do a lot of our shopping here. When I first used to visit the market I used to sit in the middle of the where the roundabout is now on the round benches and got to know a group of Polish people. They always used to congregate there. We used to meet each week. There were about ten or so of them in those days, they always had some very interesting stories to tell. They were all very cheerful chaps and I used to look forward to my weekly meeting with them. A few weeks ago when I was in here I met their self appointed leader and he told me their numbers were dwindling as there was only two of the original people left now, all the others had died over the last fifteen years. It's all very sad."

Dave Davies– Looks like rain Oh Dear!

Apart from being a great bloke, Dave was also the face of Walt Jabsco, the 2-Tone man during the market's 2-Tone 30th Anniversary event. He is also a big supporter of the market.

Dave said, "When I was young I used to come in the market with my Gran and aunty. I remember there were always loads of food stalls and fresh fruit and veg. That was in the late 50's. There was always something different to look at and I found it an exciting place. One Christmas when I was about 6 or 7 I remember they had a Father Christmas with elves and a real reindeer" he continues, "children in those days had never seen a reindeer. I really loved that. I remember the reindeer relieving itself much to the dismay of everyone present."

"Being a rude boy at the time I bought my Brutus and Ben Sherman shirts from the market. I still have a Brutus shirt now that was bought here, sadly it no longer fits! I have had some great days in the market. Now it has become an icon for tourist and we cannot afford to lose it."

Dave as Walt, below and as himself above.

A special place, Darren Ingram

Darren Ingram was born 1970 an ex-Coventry Kid is now living in Larsmo, Finland.

"The market was always a special place as a child or perhaps it is just a strong memory, as it seemed I was there so often with my mother. The different sounds of the market, the smells (both good and bad), the mass of customers (particularly when you are small, seeing these 'giants' bustling by) and the 'poor old fish' lying on the slab, the 'fields' of fruit and veg and of course, the dog charity collection boxes remain quite fresh in my mind even decades later.

In the run up to Christmas it was a great place to find those small presents that small children like inflicting on family members and the 10p stall was a particular distraction and addiction.

The strong intonation from my mother about "where to go" if I should get lost, the occasional ringing of the loud bell when another child wandered off and waiting for my mother when I was bored in the centre of the market are also strong memories. Trying to peer down to the bowels of the market through the rubbish chute (even though it had a special smell) or through the circular steps by the inspector's office, a peak into a forbidden world, must have been a sign of my inquisitiveness that would remain in my career later on as a journalist.

And I never did get to go down that access ramp by the old market toilets where those magical lorries went. Oh, was I so envious."

Johnny Twite-The Bell Man
Photo courtesy of The Coventry Telegraph

Cllr Gary Ridley
Cabinet Member for City Development

Thinking about the place I couldn't help but recall my own memories of going there for the first time with my Nan in around about 1983/4 time and coming across the fish market which looked very strange to a small boy. The smell has stayed with me ever since! The Market is a great asset for the City and seems to go from strength to strength attracting 70,000 people through the door every week!

Councillor Gary Ridley gets collared by Laurel & Hardy at the Market's 50th Gala party above and below opening the Market's mini cinema.

Birthday Greetings

21st Birthday Celebrations

The 1979 cake, an exact copy of it was used for the 40th Celebrations too.

In 1979 Coventry Market celebrated its 21st Birthday and as has become traditional, a huge cake resembling the Market was the centre-piece of the day. Instead of the traders and shoppers getting a slice, the whole thing was handed over to the children's wards at Gulson Hospital and Coventry and Warwickshire Hospital. Though the sherry apparently flowed like water at the market on the day.

Nursing Officer Pamela Hayling along with The Lord Mayor Harry Richards and Arthur Frith President of the National Market Traders Federation were at the ceremony. As were several former members of the City Council's planning Committee which had been responsible for the creation of the market. Interesting to note that in 1979 at least 30 of the original 169 traders were still going strong in the market.

40th Anniversary

The 40th Anniversary of the market in 1998 was a slightly lower key affair than the subsequent 50th, though the celebrations did last a whole month. The birthday cake was pretty spectacular, modelled as it was on the market, complete with somewhat incredible model cars on it's roof. There was Punch & Judy, Line dancing and even Coventry legend John Spencer was on hand to MC the event along with his Nostalgics dance band. The month of events ended with a spectacular laser light show. The cake was cut by Lord Mayor Cllr Maggie Rosher, with Market Traders Association Chairman Clive Miller and Market Manager Mick Finnegan.

The talk of the time was of the £1.3 million redecoration scheme and 15 stalls lost, but with 211 still remaining. Indeed the feeling was one of quiet optimism with Market Traders Association Chairman Clive Miller saying, "The future looks brighter than it has for the past ten years". He went on to say, "There's a new confidence between ourselves, the city council and London property developers Arrowcroft, who are to become our new landlords if the Lower Precinct development, which includes a covered walkway, goes ahead. 108 market traders formally withdrew their objections to the Arrowcroft proposal, which involved the council slapping a compulsory purchase order on the market hall in November the year before. This gave the £33 million scheme the green light although nightclub Mr George's, The Co-op and Kwick Save all raised objections. History tells us that it went ahead in any case and the Lower Precinct got a make-over that I personally think worked very well. My only gripe is that I think such an area should be used far more than it is. It's outside and undercover, cafe culture should be huge".

The then market traders chairman Clive Miller, with Lord Mayor Cllr Maggie Rosher and Market Manager Mick Finnigan and the anniversary cake.
Photo courtesy of the Coventry Telegraph

BUCKINGHAM PALACE

30th October, 2008

Dear Mr. Duffin,

I have been asked to thank you, the Traders, Management and Staff of Coventry Retail Market for your kind letter containing loyal greetings to The Queen, sent on the occasion of your Gala Dinner which is being held on 8th November to mark the Fiftieth Anniversary of the opening of your Market building, which replaced the one destroyed during the Blitz.

Her Majesty much appreciates your thoughtfulness in writing as you did and, in return, sends her warm, good wishes to all those who will be present at the dinner for a most memorable and enjoyable event.

Yours sincerely,

Sonia Bonici

Mrs Sonia Bonici
Senior Correspondence Officer

William B. Duffin, Esq.

Fifty Glorious Years

In November 2008 Coventry Market celebrated fifty years. As to be expected the event was going to be something memorable and very special. A celebration gala was planned, along with a Birthday event that would see the market in wall to wall celebration. Eclipsing all this though was something unique and somewhat off the wall, Coventry Market The Musical.

BBC Coventry & Warwickshire were the movers behind the project and the plan was to have the Market traders and shoppers taking part in a song that would be filmed and premiered on the night of the Tuesday 4th November, the market's 50th Birthday. Composer and filmmaker Benjamin Till headed up the project with months of work and auditions actually taking place in the market's own BBC Coventry & Warwickshire stall.

The big day began slowly, with everyone setting their stalls up. I was there with my wife Julie, selling my 2-Tone books and as part of the day, the market had kindly funded a wonderful Fender Telecaster deluxe guitar, that I got signed by the Specials. Everyone who bought my book stood a chance to win it in the prize draw, as the last event in the market on the day. There were fruit and vegetables at 1958 prices and Chitty Chitty Bang Bang (complete with the Lord and Lady Mayor). Celebrity chef Rusty Lee was on hand with her infectious laugh and culinary know-how taking part in a Caribbean breakfast. You knew she was there of course and as the day kicked in, the market started filling up and ubiquitous work men came past carrying things that you had no idea what they could be used for. By 10.00am the feeling of calm had been replaced by blind panic and the place filled with expectant shoppers, all looking to bag a bargain. Although it was only fruit and vegetables from a selected stall that offered 1958 prices, it didn't stop some over expectant punters wanting everything in the building at the same deal. I can tell you it's hard breaking the news to a lady who had walked nearly two miles with a shopping trolley that the turkey she had so set her heart on was not for sale for 5/6.

The Great British public are great on days like this, we had our stall all neatly laid out, everything in it's place and a place for everything, then someone would come along and kindly rearrange our displays for no logical reason. Often not speaking in the process and walk away like the last three minutes of their lives never happened. We had requests of all sorts, "No, we are only selling 2-Tone books here, you're after the vegetable stall over there".

It was great fun, and MC Andy held it altogether, as the local media descended on the stall holders to ask them the same questions that the last media guy had just posed. The mood from the traders was good though and the rumour is no customers were ritually sacrificed that day at all!

Come 5pm and the activity around our stall increased as the Specials guitar draw neared, especially when Special Bass guitarist Horace Panter arrived. This was mid way through the 'will they ,won't they' reform debate, and Horace had just told me that things 'were' going to happen at long last. So I was in good spirit when the draw took place, we expected a few redraws to be honest, as you had to be present to claim the amazing six-stringed prize. To our amazement the first ticket Horace picked out was the winner (Andy Gailey) and a winner who was not only present, but had bought a second ticket just an hour before, although it was a previous one he had won with. As the huge crowd of people and media began to depart, we were slightly sad that our part of the day had now ended and something we had planned for some time had now concluded.

That wasn't the end of the celebrations by any means of course, enter stage two and it was the market's talents turn to shine. The Sherbourne Mall walkway from the market to Lower Precinct was bedecked with a rather long red carpet befitting a premier. This was the very first showing of Coventry Market the Musical and it was going out live on BBC Midlands Today news and BBC Coventry & Warwickshire Radio. That was evident by the BBC's version of mission control running along the side of the seating area. No one really knew what to expect and I wasn't planning on being impressed, but the whole thing actually worked and Coventry Market showed that it was more than a shopping experience once again. The project was nominated for a SONY but sadly didn't win. Just being nominated is proof (if it were needed) that the whole thing was very much worthwhile and got all the right reactions.

Following the Market's 50th came the Market Gala Dinner at Coventry's Britannia Hotel. Another lively event made the merrier with the addition of a Marilyn Monroe and Laurel and Hardy lookalikes. The two guys were hilarious especially their piano-shifting exploits. Great crowd and great food for a great reason.

109

COVENTRY MARKET
THE MUSICAL!
BBC COVENTRY & WARWICKSHIRE

Above BBC presenter Liz Kershaw gets things rolling, with 'mission control' in the foreground. Left, the red carpet, below the Market the musical goes 'big screen'.

Gala Night with a few
famous faces and
Marilyn Monroe and
Laurel and Hardy

The 50th Birthday party. Top left Rusty Lee, top right the guitar is nearly won: the author, MC Andy and Special Horace Panter. Below left the stilt-walker broke a leg, bottom right Market manager Brian Sexton with Sophie and Bill Duffin of Shoekings. Middle Veg at 1958 prices.

You'll Never Believe Who Was Here

The Iron Lady visits Coventry Market with press and film crew (and son Mark *extreme right*).

Photograph courtesy of the Coventry Telegraph

In 1976 leader of the opposition Margaret Thatcher, made a visit to the Market along with her son Mark (hope he didn't get lost).

She had been leader of the Conservative Party for a year and would have to wait three years before she became Britain's first female Prime Minister. Around the time of her visit she made the key speech ("Britain Awake") attacking the Soviet Union, claiming the Russians were bent on world dominance and put guns before butter. The Soviet Defence Ministry responded and called her 'The Iron Lady', a nickname that would stick throughout her career, though she took delight in the name and it's unwavering and steadfast qualities.

Jamie Oliver – Out of the stalls too early

In August 2000, celebrity TV chef Jamie Oliver visited Coventry Market. It should have been a glorious affair for all concerned, the problem was, he turned up on the wrong day!

The visit was filmed as part of his TV show "The Naked Chef". The idea was to show students how they could make a good cheap meal from ingredients sourced from the market. The chef got his days mixed up and instead of arriving to a prepared welcoming committee on the Tuesday, he got there a day ahead on a rather quiet Monday.

Market Manager Michael Finnegan said at the time, "He just turned up out of the blue, he had his days mixed up, he apologised and we gave him the market tour anyway. Even though he caught us by surprise, he still found time to talk to a good few of the customers and traders. He signed a lot of autographs and came over as a nice lad".

On the day Jamie's shopping list included a leg of pork, English stick beans, potatoes, apricots, coriander and fennel seeds. He was looking for cut-price produce and he found it at PJ Reid butcher's stall. He asked Stall Manager Graham Hartopp if he gave students discount, "I gave him a fiver off, because we usually knock something off for the students".

He also visited Rhema Spice stall and spoke to Jayne Hodson, who remembers the chef visiting the market once before (presumably on the right day). She said that he told her it was a good little market and he liked the variety of the stalls.

Big Brother's Bex & Luke visit to Coventry

Saturday 23rd August 2008

brought to you by the **Coventry Telegraph**

Autograph

Autograph

To the Market Manager xx

Luke x

Thanks for the fun!

in association with

Precinct

Coventry Market

Celebrating 50 years

Above-Doors, What doors? Below, the Mural.

MISCELLANY

In the market for prizes

Over the years Coventry Market has given away some pretty spectacular prizes. In 1998 to celebrate their 40th anniversary the market held a competition to win a Coventry-built Peugeot 206 car worth £15,000. Despite having no driving licence market regular (and keen cyclist) Brenda Garrod won the car, but by all accounts kept on cycling to the market.

Brenda and her car.

Some years later it was a snazzy EP-X Roadster bicycle worth £1,500 up for grabs as part of a promotion for the city's Tech Festival. Market Manager Brian Sexton was delighted with the huge response the competition got and it was finally won by Andy Brown. The prize was handed over by Brian and Natasha Beetison of EP-X.

From Let to Right, Brian Sexton, the winner Andy Brown and Natasha Beetison.

Photo courtesy of the Coventry Telegraph

Now Showing-The World's Smallest Cinema

Market Manager Brian Sexton has a canny ability to capture the imagination and create ideas that work well. Though in August 2009, even he was a little surprised when his idea to have the world's smallest cinema in the Market caught the imagination of just about everyone.

It little matters if it actually is the smallest or not. What's important is the huge interest it brings to the Market. The Coventry Telegraph got into it big time and did a fact file on other pigmy picture houses, including a one-seater in Amsterdam, enough said. No matter, the Market Cinema was a box office hit and made column inches in the Daily Mirror, The Sun and The Metro, even coaxing Central TV out to have a peek.

Market Manager Brian Sexton had this to say about this cinematic marvel. "We have commissioned films about the market in the last thirteen years, one for 40th birthday and the famous Coventry Market the Musical, for the 50th birthday celebrations. Many people have never had a chance to watch them, so how do you get people to watch them, you put them in a cinema and so we have built our very own Market Cinema for that purpose. It's a two seater but we can bring in a couple more seats if it gets busy" he joked. Brian continued, "We are hoping that people will pop in for ten minutes here and there during their shopping trips, maybe buy an ice cream from the stall next door and enjoy our films. It's a two hour loop, so the chances of seeing repeated footage is not very likely, but it gives people a chance to see the story and social history that has been made about the market".

It was officially opened on 14th August 2009 by Councillor Gary Ridley with the films showing on a loop of "Coventry Market - The Musical", "Around Market People", "I Could Have been a Boring Factory Worker" and "Notes Around 50".

Councillor Ridley cuts the ribbon.

Making Movies

The maker of most of the films showing at the market cinema is a familiar face around the place, Alan Van Wijgerden. His films have a stark realism about them, never in your face, but always filmed with an honesty that never fails to bring the message across. It's Alan's superb quality films that will help pin-point moments in time, in the life of this huge arena of retail.

I put some questions to Alan about his spectacular film work.

Pete Chambers-How many films have you made for/about the market, and what are they called and how long did each take to make?
Alan Van Wijgerden-I've made three films for the market., The first was called "Around Market People" and took two years to complete, being finished in 2000. It's 16 minutes long, black and white and colour and was shot on 16mm film. The second film completed for the fiftieth is called "Notes Around Fifty". The third film is the feature called "I Could Have Been a Boring Factory Worker". So far as I know it's the only independently produced documentary feature finished in the region in about the last three years. The feature also took two years to complete.

PC-What makes the market tick for you?
AVW-I was taken around the market as a small child by my parents and I've shopped there all my adult life. In 1998 I was buying pickled herrings from one of the fishmongers in the market, (the only one in town you can buy them loose from, and bigger than you get in the little supermarket jars) when the topic of the fortieth anniversary came up. One of the stallholders said "It won't be here in another forty years". So I thought why not make a doc about Coventry Market. That was the start of what's now been a twelve year involvement with the market and its people.

PC-What are your cinematic influences?
AVW-The key influence on my filmmaking has always been the Free Cinema movement, in particular its directors Lindsay Anderson, Karel Reisz and Tony Richardson, the leaders of the British Social Realism movement of the nineteen sixties. One of Lindsay's early films was "Every Day Except Christmas," a film about London's Covent Garden Market, now a tourist attraction, a film that I've always admired. The Free Cinema manifesto says:- No film can be too personal. The image speaks. Sound amplifies and comments. Perfection is not an aim. A style means an attitude an attitude means a style. But mostly with me it's an interest in the poetry of the everyday.

2-Tone Market

Right from the start there has been a 2-tone connection with Coventry Market, have a look at the BBC produced film for Concrete Jungle, and you'll see that a lot of it takes place around the perimeter of the Market. Midnight, the record stall (that's very Paul Taylor to you and me), has been selling 2-Tone badges, patches and T-shirts for over ten years in the market and still is. Not to mention some very sought after 2-Tone vinyl. Fast forward 30 years and the market is a safe-bet if you want to have a close encounter of the 2-Tone kind. Former Swinging Cat and Special AKA guitarist John Shipley is a regular in the place he's the man who provided the music to Alan Wijgerden's "Coventry Market At Fifty" film. During the 2008 market 50th birthday celebrations, I was asked to do a couple of book signings of my book 2-Tone-2, this included the giving away of a Fender guitar to one lucky winner (Andy Gailey) signed by the whole band, with Specials bass master Horace Panter doing the honours. 2009 began with the unveiling of the very first 2-Tone plaque by Specials Roddy Byers and Horace Panter at the Canal Basin, sponsored by the market. These plaques commemorated 30 years of this thought provoking music in the city of its birth and were located at important sites pertinent to 2-Tones history. The Canal Basin was the setting for the iconic cover shots of the first two Specials albums.

Through the best part of 2009 there stood the 2-Tone Market Exhibition on the Heritage Stall, a fascinating collection of ska memorabilia that saw an amazing amount

The Market Heritage stall during its 2-Tone period.

of visitors coming along to see it. It was to form the backbone of the 30th Birthday of 2-Tone celebrated in the market as part of my 2-Tone @ 30 campaign. The day proved to be a splendid 2-Tone family day out with children all decked out in their finest black and white. It was great to see and personally I saw it symbolic of the legacy of 2-Tone music being handed down to the next generation to enjoy. It made certain that this important anniversary in musical history was not missed.

Also on the day 2 Tone City Clothing opened for business, run by Steve and Linzi Eaton. The stall is a veritable Aladdin's cave of skinhead, rude boy and retro attire, plus badges, ska and reggae CD's and everything else you can think of. Steve or 'Cardboard' to his friends was the gentleman who is seen on the front cover of the first Selecter album "Too Much Pressure". His DJ sets have become legendary, not to mention his (and wife Linzi's) fascinating stories of life in the fast lane of ska. Sadly they closed their stall in September 2009.

When Midlands Ska band The Allskas wanted a location for the cover of their first single "In Our Coventry Home", they chose to do it in The Market Parlour, the market stall I had been using to research this very book. Decked out like a 1950's living room, it proved just the right setting for the cover of their charity single and

Steve Cardboard recreated his Selecter cover pose especially for the cover photo. The band incidentally included guest vocalist Aitch Bembridge from the Selecter and the Specials and Irena Bosworth. Irena is not only a member of the Allskas, but many will know her from the market's Computer Corner stall and her other band The Phoenix Rock 'N' Roll band. The band also includes Computer Corner's other trader, drummer extraordinaire Graham Clarke. Meanwhile Dave West a familiar face on the markets key cutting stall, also has strong links with the genre, he was a member of the Bonediggers and band fronted by Specials guitarist Roddy 'Radiation' Byers. Dave now fronts his new band the intriguingly titled 'Men Dressed As Men'.

Aitch opens 2-Tone City clothing for Steve and Linzi, now sadly closed.

2-Tone Trail plaque number four (located at the Rocket pub to celebrate the Horizon studio site adjacent) was kindly sponsored by Bill Duffin from the Shoekings stall, who along with the Market Traders Association sponsored the aforementioned charity single by the Allskas "In Our Coventry Home". The CD was launched at the Rocket following the plaque unveiling, with Nev Staple from The Specials and Buster Bloodvessel from Bad Manners doing the honours.

In the future I am working to see that the ideas that began with great effect with the markets 2-tone Exhibition, become something bigger and more permanent, hopefully located in the Market, so I am hoping that 2010 we will see a 2-Tone museum become a reality.

The bowels of the Market

While the market's main floor is pretty well known to most Coventry folk, there is a part of the market that stays for the best part hidden from public view. This area is right under your feet and is the basement, where the waste compactor whirls away and where those market traders disappear to when they tell you "they may have one in the lock-up", though some traders don't even like going there.

The basement is not the sort of place you would want to spend the night in, it's very spooky and the story goes that it is haunted. It obviously occupies the same dimensions as the market's retail floor, it's here where the traders have their storerooms. It's also here where those chutes in the centre of the market lead to, where all the waste is collected into huge skips to be taken away.

The place looks like some-sort of archaic prison, as you walk past the various rooms in the half-light, you almost expect to hear the moans of tortured souls, locked in a bleak timeless void. It's never very light and there's a eerie silence about the place. It's so grim that it was often used as a practice area by the fire services. Though I'm surprised it has never been used in a film, it would make an ideal location, maybe they should do guided tours down there, especially now it's listed.

So the next time your in the market, you may like to think about what's under your feet, probably best not to think too hard though.

Let me out

Top, the bowels of the market, did you hear that? What was that noise, it sounded like footsteps, but there's no one else herrrrrrrrrrrrrrr.............
Below, if you ever wondered where the central garbage chute goes, well here's your answer, you can see the chute on the left, just above to the right of the fire hose.

1. The market is constructed of over 10,000 cubic yards of reinforced concrete, weighing about 18,000 tons combined with 630 tons of high tensile steel reinforcement.
2. The market is 276 feet (84.124 8 meters) in diameter .
3. The Basement level is 16 to 20 feet below the original ground level. For the remainder of the building, 282 reinforced piles were driven up to 20 feet deep (6.096 meters).
4. Refuse is emptied into chutes that lead to the basement where it is collected and disposed of.
5. The main contractors for Coventry Market were William Moss & Sons Ltd. Building and Civil Engineering Contractors, based in Loughborough.
6. Rent for a stall would have cost you £6 a week in 1958.
7. The market took £385,000 to build, including £65,000 to covert the former Cornercroft factory into the fish market.
8. The Market is the oldest trading area administered by the City Council, with it's roots going back to medieval times. The word market comes from the Latin mercatus-meaning buying selling or trade.
9. Originally markets could only be set up by royal grant.
10. The average internal height of the current market is 15 feet (4.572 meters).
11. The market is not just a place of retail, it has also been in the forefront of campaigning over the years. It collected 10,000 signatures to hold on to pensioners' bus passes for another year. In 1994 a flower decked stand was placed in the centre of the market in tribute to 68 people massacred in Sarajevo market.
12. The famous roundabout was originally owned by 'Uncle Jack' and Flora Statham and appeared on a bombed site after the war to amuse the children. In 1958 when the market opened a new roundabout was also opened.
13. In 1980 one stall sold for an amazing £24,000
14. Coventry Market was featured in the BBC sitcom "Home Time" in 2009, 'Jean the Knicker Lady' was also referenced.
15. The market hand bell was traditionally rang to attract the attention of a missing child or warning of a bomb scare.

Christmas
1962

WITH THANKS ETC

Project coordinator-Julie Chambers
Project originator-Brian Sexton
Proof Reading-Georgette Stutins
Words of wisdom-Bill Duffin
Tea and Coffee-Sophie Duffin
Words, original photography and design-Pete Chambers

With Thanks to......

Julie Chambers, Brian Sexton, Michael Finnegan, Bill and Sophie Duffin, The Market Traders Federation, Irena Bosworth, Steve Dibb, Kev Monks, Alan Van Wijgerden, The Coventry Archive, The Jerde Partnership, Coventry City Council, CV One, The Coventry Telegraph, The Coventry Observer, everyone who contributed to the book in any way and all the good people who work and shop in Coventry Market.

Websites
Coventry Market official site-www.coventrymarket.co.uk
Rupert The Fish's website-www.rupert-fish.co.uk
Alan Van Wijgerden's website-www.vanwijgerden.fsnet.co.uk